MW00597556

Discovering God's Priceless Gems
My Amazing Assignment

◆◇◆

By Pearlie I. Ealey-Forrest

DORRANCE
PUBLISHING CO
EST. 1920
PITTSBURGH, PENNSYLVANIA 15238

Dorrance Publishing Co
585 Alpha Drive
Pittsburgh, PA 15238
Visit our website at www.dorrancebookstore.com

ISBN: 978-1-6453-0259-1
eISBN: 978-1-6453-0788-4

Table of Contents

Many gems are valuable, but I discovered that God's gems, embedded in my old, torn, treasured trunk, are unique and priceless.

Dedication

To my son Mark Phillip and his wife Kelly, who helped with computer skills. They are devout believers, musicians, ministers, great leaders, and an inspiration to me.

To William Phillip Forrest, retired English professor, professional musician, and the love of my life. He has been a great influence in my life.

To my grandchildren: Crystal and her husband John, who helped with the rewriting; Freddie, Jr. and his wife Ericka, who believe in my endeavors; Karen and her husband Joseph Jamaal, who give me much enthusiasm; Darien, who is very supportive; Matthew, who is a great encourager; Vanessa and her husband Joshua, who are very caring; Mykkail, a delightful young man; Mark Phillip, Jr., a great musician; and my great-grandchildren Phillip, Freddie III, Joseph, Jr., Chloe Annette, Chloe Lynn, Aubrey Symone, Divine, and Kemar.

To the loving memories of my daughter Annette and her husband Freddie Sr., who were great inspirations to me.

This dedication is also to my niece Kimberly Joy, a high school English teacher who helped with the rewording and grammar.

To another young lady, Dashae, who assisted me with her computer skills.

To each of them I dedicate the following poem

Exposed to Reveal

Heads above the crowd,
Radiant pure delight,
Illuminates the world,
Brilliancy in sight.

Tender plants grow up,
Glories are concealed,
When fierce storms cease,
Beauty is revealed.

Heads above the crowd,
Appearances aren't odd,
Exposed to reveal,
Marvelous works of God.

Introduction
Discovering God's Priceless Gems

The discoveries are always fresh and have astounded me through the years. Many gems are valuable, but the gems which came from the discovery in my old, torn, trunk have given me the awesome desire to pursue all that God has for me.

This book is about various encounters that inspired me to tell others about the God who is "no respecter of persons" He is anxious to know each person. These encounters took place:

> in my home with family, friends, neighbors, and classmates;
> at work with co-workers, supervisors, and clients;
> during visits to hospitals and nursing homes;
> in public places like restaurants;
> during after-school tutoring programs for "at risk" students;
> during telephone conversations;
> and the list goes on.

My Journey

This book is my extensive journey of presenting the "Plan of Salvation." Most of these converts were face-to-face encounters. Several of these same converts introduced their family members, co-workers and friends to me so that they, too, could accept Jesus personally and/or be filled with the Holy Spirit. The ones I could not meet in person prayed the prayer of salvation via telephone.

My Weekly Television Program

While living in Cincinnati, Ohio, I had a weekly Bible-teaching television program. At the close of each program, I asked the television audience to pray to receive Jesus as Savior if they had not done so previously.

The program ran for four years and was successful. I closed it when I retired and moved 700 miles to a city where television access was very limited. However, my greatest joy in witnessing was in-person.

The Work Continues

Now, I am a senior citizen living in an independent retirement home. The work still goes on. I teach a weekly Bible class of encouragement to other occupants. I also do a quarterly publication. I enjoy my fellowship with God, and the witnessing continues.

What Should Readers Take Away From This Book?

If you do not know Jesus personally, He desires for you to accept Him. If you are a "Born Again" believer, share your experiences with others. If you have not received the gift of the Holy Spirit, read Acts chapter two and ask the Holy Spirit to fill you with Himself. Parents and grandparents, tell your children and grandchildren about the saving power of Jesus Christ and allow them to accept Him personally.

If you are employed, share your God-given experiences with co-workers.

Tell your friends or those you come in contact with about the love of Jesus.

Tell family members, including those out of state, about Jesus. Be humble, not arrogant, in your presentation, and kindly share your experiences and walk with the Lord Jesus Christ. Use every opportunity available to present the "Plan of Salvation."

A Poem I Wrote to Explain my Journey

DIRECTION
Before the break of dawn,
Bowed my head to pray,
Sought His perfect will,
My mission to fulfill.

Searched His precious truth,
Read His awesome word,
My faith is on release,
For God's amazing peace.

Order my steps dear Lord,
Illuminate my way,
In Your divine will,
Purposes, I'll fulfill.

Mountain peaks, I seek,
For a better view,
Reaching out to others,
My sisters and my brothers.

◆◇◆

Other books by Pearlie I. Ealey-Forrest:

God Knows the Way that I Take (autobiography, currently out of print)

Biography of father Jeremiah Ealey *Are All of the Children Inside? (biography of father Jeremiah Ealey*, amazon.com)

Both books were printed by Xlibris and copyrighted in 2008.

Chapter 1

SECRET OF OLD TIN TRUNK

An old worn tin trunk, given to me by my mother, sat near my bed. Personal turmoil in the big city had forced me to return to my parents' home in my hometown. I felt as hideous as the old trunk. *Was the answer to my future embedded in that trunk?* I didn't know the answer I sought would give me amazing insight that would lead me to a wonderful future. It would also lead me on a path to reveal this insight to my siblings and countless others.

I stared at the trunk for a while before reopening it. Searching through old school records, small booklets, and notes of disappointment, I discovered a special small book. About two years earlier, while living in Cincinnati, Ohio, I had watched a program on TV and sent for a book entitled *How to Find God*, which the preacher announced at the end of the program. I had never heard of evangelist Billy Graham. So when his book arrived, I had packed it in the old tin trunk. This day, the book caught my attention. *Is God the answer?*

My parents were devout Christians. Daddy, now elderly, was a preacher and had pastored a church. He and my mother read the Bible and prayed with us. However, they had not led us in a prayer to accept Jesus Christ personally. "Perhaps this little book, *How to Find God*, will give me some answers," I whispered to myself. I decided to read the book, fast, and pray. My mother often fasted when she was seeking an answer from God.

I worked for a private family. Since I was fasting, I was glad that cooking was not one of my duties. Tuesday after work, I laid across my bed, opened the book, and began to read. "Who is God? What is He like? How can I know He exists? Where did He begin? Can I know Him?" These are some of the questions evangelist Graham asked. *This is interesting.*

Evangelist Graham followed his question with some of the most descriptive adjectives I had ever known. Beautiful pictures of God's magnificent universe laid before me. Countless stars, the moon, and the sun were uniquely designed. Something holds them intact. We are daily faced with these miracles.

Evangelist Graham went on to tell how the law of gravity holds everything in their proper places. I had marveled at the universe while traveling in different parts of the South. These were the clay hills of Georgia. Tall pines, gigantic oaks, and the woodlands were amazing. Mountains and valleys of North Carolina, South Carolina, Tennessee, and Kentucky were also breathtaking.

What about God? As long as I could remember, God's name was constantly spoken in our home. Daddy and Mother addressed God at the beginning and close of each day. Prayer was a daily way of life. They sang about Him. It appeared that God was the unseen guest at our table. Yet, I didn't know Him. Evangelist Graham stated that there are countless people who have some form of emotional experience and say they are born again. However, their lifestyles do not correspond with God's requirements in His Word, the Holy Bible.

I wanted to read more of *How to Find God*, but it had gotten late in the night. The next day would be a busy workday. I placed a marker between the pages, closed the book, and fell asleep.

Wednesday morning, I began my fast and went to work. All day, as I did laundry and cleaned my employer's house, phrases out of *How to Find God* lingered in my mind. It was a joyful day, and more joy than I had experienced in a very long time. I wanted to know Jesus Christ (God's Son) in a personal way."

Chapter 2

THE GIANT SCREEN

The moment I asked Jesus to be my Savior, a giant movie screen appeared before me. It seemed so real, as if I could touch it. Yet, I laid still and focused on the view. It seemed to be set in motion.

A tall mountain stood before me. A large, endless river flowed between the mountain and me. The sky above was light blue. It caused the waters to appear blue. However, I realized the waters were clear. There was not a speck of debris anywhere.

What is this? I thought, as I viewed the big screen, which was almost tangible in my bedroom. It was revealed to me that God was telling me about my past and current situations. I was twenty-three years of age and had given Him the privilege of washing my sins away. One day I will enjoy eternal life with Him.

My mind took me back to my past. I was approximately nine years of age and stood near an old cedar tree. Suddenly, a picture of a medium-sized book, about four-by-five inches in width and length and one-inch thick, appeared before me. Even though I was a child, it was revealed to me that this was the amount of sins I had committed after becoming knowledgeable of my wrongdoings.

My father was a preacher, and my mother was also a dedicated Christian. Because of their strict teachings, after I turned about seven years of age, I knew the rights and wrongs of everyday life. Nevertheless, I didn't know how to ask Jesus to come into my life and be my Savior. Now, I had come to realize that children can come into the accountability of their sins under ten years of age. Later, I would become involved in seeing small children, seven years of age and older, give their lives to Jesus Christ, including my own two children.

Let's return to the giant movie screen. From the time I was ten years of age to age twenty-three, my sins had increased from a medium-sized book to a gigantic mountain. Yet, God washed my sins away. I told my father and mother of my encounter with God and how my sins had been washed away. They rejoiced with me.

The movie picture scene has never left my mind. In fact, it helped prepare me to witness to many, many people. After God ended the movie, *Giant Screen*, I thought about the treasure I had pulled out of the old, worn tin trunk. It was a gem that would produce gems. An inspired book, *How to Find God*, by His faithful servant Dr. Billy Graham, had produced the miracle.

Eighteen years later, I would be given the opportunity to be a counselor at one of Dr. Billy Graham's crusades in Cincinnati, Ohio. However, this experience would have to wait. I felt the call of God to share my "born again," experience with others now. Although a little fearful, this would not stop me from obeying and honoring the God who had just saved me from my sins. Timid, but here I come!

Chapter 3

TIMID, BUT AVAILABLE

I was excited about my new experience with God. It appeared that His amazing love overwhelmed me. It was time to share. *But, who will listen to a young lady in her early twenties?*

In my small hometown of approximately 400 people, many did not profess to be Christians and demonstrated it by their lifestyles. Those thirty years and older knew when I was born. Many of these townspeople knew of my parents' strict rules but often tried to persuade me to try their lifestyles. "Going to church on Sunday is okay, but after church service and during the week we do what we want to do, as long as we do not break the law," they stated. However, as long as my siblings and I were under our parents' supervision, we obeyed them.

I felt a deep urge to witness to an elderly man I had known all of my life. Some of his grandchildren and I attended the same school. Uncle G was a known alcoholic. He never attended church and used foul language. During the day, he usually sat on the porch of his "shack," as most people called his dilapidated house. He lived near the grocery and supply stores. We always spoke as we passed his house, and he responded kindly.

Late one morning, I approached his house. As usual, he was seated on his porch. "Good morning, Uncle G. How are you?" I asked kindly.

"All right," he replied. I said a few complimentary words and began talking about the goodness of God. He became quiet.

"Do you know Jesus personally?" I asked.

In a gruff voice, he responded, "I was saved before the foundation of the world, and have always known the Lord." He repeated himself a few times.

I eased away feeling very defeated. *Was my approach wrong? Why did I offend him?* At this time I had not been to Bible school and had no lessons on how to share my experience of having a personal relationship with Jesus Christ. But, I had the urge to share that particular day. Deep within my mind, I knew that there were other people who needed to be asked the same question.

I was proud of my little book, *How to Find God*, and often took it with me.

Most of the time, my work was in private families' homes. One day, as I sat at the table eating lunch, I read my book.

"Do you have another one of those books?" my employer asked.

"No, I do not," was my reply.

Months later, when I had gone to another job, the lady who had asked for the book, *How to Find God*, came to mind. "I should have given her the book, since I have given my life to God," I whispered. I had missed the opportunity to carry out another assignment.

Then, there was the young "Professor," as most called him. He played for church choirs and was the high school English teacher and choir director at Tattnall County Industrial High School. He taught my four sisters and youngest brother. One afternoon, I stopped by his house and began a conversation about the Lord. "Do you know Jesus personally?" I asked. He appeared to be a little insulted and talked about the wonderful work he did. This time, I was not frightened. The strong urging of the Lord had been there, and I knew it.

Years later, this teacher became a part of our family. You are right! He prayed "The Sinner's Prayer" with me. "Professor" is now ninety-three years of age and really loves the Lord. He is one of the musicians at the church I attend. However, my assignment had only begun. Young people weighed heavily on my mind. *Ages seven through ten is a good place to start.*

Chapter 4

THE SPLENDOR OF YOUNG PEOPLE

My mother began Community Bible Study for Young People. Each Sunday afternoon, they came to our house, sat on the front porch, and listened to teachings about the love of Jesus. There were representatives from most of the religions in our small town.

Soon, the young people's Bible study became my responsibility. I moved the class to the church I attended. We met on Friday nights, and I taught different parts of the Bible, making it applicable to young people. During the summer, we took trips to Tybee Beach and Jekyll Island in Georgia. Some of our favorite beaches were Hilton Head, South Carolina and Fernandina Beach, Florida. During autumn, winter ,and spring, we had special programs, which were always held on Friday nights.

In 1960, my father went to his permanent home with the Lord. I continued teaching the young people. In the summer of 1963, Mother, my six-year-old daughter Annette, and I moved to Cincinnati, Ohio. The young people and I cried many tears. However, someone capable took over the classes.

Mother and I began Community Bible Study for Young People in Avondale, a community in Cincinnati. Many young people, teens, and preteens, came to the classes and gave their lives to Jesus Christ.

One Halloween night, while Mother and I passed out bags of candy, many young people came. They were the love and joy of our lives and enjoyed our home. While they tarried for a while, Mother and I shared the story of Jesus.

Many of all ages gave their lives to Jesus. My daughter Annette was among the group. She lived a godly lifestyle through grade school, high school, college, and beyond.

A pastor once spoke of a church official who approached him about his sermons. While preaching, the pastor encouraged young people to give their lives to God. He would tell them that God would forgive their confessed sins. The church official said, "Pastor, please don't call our young people's mistakes sin. It embarrasses them and offends some parents." The pastor was silent, so the official continued. "Can't you just say that they used poor judgment?"

Walking over to the corner of his office, the pastor took a bottle from a high shelf. It was used to kill insects, and the label on the bottle read, "Poison." He walked back and stood in front of the official. "Would you like for me to change the label on this bottle to read, 'Essence of Peppermint?' Do you feel that I should replace the true label with a false one, so as to not embarrass or offend anyone?" he asked.

The pastor continued, "Romans 3:23, 'All have sinned and come short of the glory of God.' Romans 6:23, 'The wages of sin is death, but the gift of God is eternal life through Jesus Christ our Lord.' John 3:16, 'For God so loved the world, that He gave His only begotten Son, that whosoever believeth in Him should not perish but have everlasting life.'"

I believed, like this pastor, and set forth to witness to people of all ages, from six years of age and older, or when they became aware of right from wrong. Another kind of assignment was given, which puzzled me. In most cases, I could not be biased in my street witnessing. So, my prayer life increased.

Chapter 5

KNOCK ON EVERY DOOR

While living in Avondale, the United States' general election was coming up. One of the campaign managers of that area asked me to pass out literature endorsing a particular political party. "Knock on every door!" he said. I suggested that he give me specific details for my assignment. He continued, "Ask all of those who are eighteen years of age and older to vote for candidates who are running for an office in this party. If they are not registered to vote, they have time to go and register. I am giving you these streets to canvass." He gave me a list of the streets. He was kind, but very direct in his assignment.

After I left his presence, four words echoed in my mind, "Knock on every door!" I realized that some would probably criticize the candidate and even the party with harsh words. However, I couldn't allow their criticism to deter me. My approach and requests would be persuasive but calm. To my surprise, no one was harsh with their words or emotions. They received the literature.

After the election, I knew that God wanted me to continue with the assignment He had given me. "Knock on every door" did not mean for me to go to everyone's house, but to use every available opportunity He provided to tell others about His amazing love and will for their lives. "For I know the thoughts that I think toward you, says the Lord, thoughts of peace, and not of evil, to give you an expected end," Jeremiah 29:11.

Most of my witnessing had been to children and young people, but I felt the urge of the Lord to do more. One day, I went with a group of ladies to a

Bible study at Catherine's house in downtown Cincinnati. Catherine was about forty years of age and a double amputee. Her caretaker welcomed us in as Catherine cheerfully bounced around in her wheelchair. It puzzled me that she was so joyful. Her husband was a hard worker and had hired someone to take care of his wife during the day.

There were several abandoned houses on her street. Their house was very frail. I am sure it was difficult to heat during the winter when the ice and snow fell. There was no central heating or air conditioning. It was quite warm when we were there, but Catherine never complained.

About an hour later, the Bible study concluded. "Please come back," Catherine pleaded. We went to our separate homes, but Catherine was on my mind. A few weeks later, I went back to Catherine's. I knew she loved the Lord, but I witnessed to her caretaker. As I walked down the street to take a bus home, the echo resounded in my mind, "Knock on every door." I noticed that someone lived in a very old, frail house. Courage grabbed hold of me, and I knocked. The door was opened. "Come on in." The voice came from an old man at the end of the hallway. "I am blind. Can't see anything," he said. I witnessed to him and quickly made my way out.

That elderly, blind man stayed on my mind. When I went back to see him, my sister Ethel Pearl joined me. After knocking on the door, we were invited in. Another old man sat in a corner. "I can see better than I could yesterday," the blind man stated.

A few days later, I thought about what he had said. "I can see better." Was God restoring his sight? I guess I will never know because I did not return to his house. The street was littered with alcoholic cans and bottles and mounds of paper. This made me fearful.

My community witnessing was put on hold, but I knew God would continue to use me. However, there was a very important event coming up that most young ladies long for.

Chapter 6

INTERMISSION

On December 24, 1966, I was married to William Phillip Forrest. He was the high school music and English professor I had witnessed to six years earlier. We were married in Cincinnati even though he resided in Georgia and taught at the high school near his home. After a week's honeymoon, he returned to his teaching position in Georgia. A couple months later, the Tattnall County Board of Education allowed him to cancel his contract and move to Cincinnati. He applied for a position as an English teacher at a school near the apartment complex where we lived. About three weeks later, he was hired.

We attended church regularly. In fact, William was the church's musician. We purchased a home in the beautiful neighborhood of Bond Hill in Cincinnati when our son was about one-month old and our daughter Annette was ten years of age. A couple months later, I became extremely ill with a death sentence hanging over me and was hospitalized for approximately three weeks. Nevertheless, God miraculously healed me, for I still had much work to do for Him.

William and I both worked when the children were small, so I didn't do much witnessing until I became employed as an investigator at the Hamilton County Department in downtown Cincinnati. I heard the echo again, "Knock on every door! Use every available opportunity to witness!"

The intermission was over. I knew without a shadow of a doubt that I would be giving 100-plus percent of dedicated service as an investigator. However, before my witnessing assignment could continue, I had to take an advanced course in witnessing training. Would I pass the course?

Chapter 7

DEFEAT TO TRIUMPH

I had an overwhelming desire to speak to Mr. H. about the love of God and His plan for our salvation. He lived about two blocks from me. At the time, there was no evidence in his lifestyle or conversation that revealed he knew God personally. Yet, his wife showed signs of salvation.

I was off from work and my seven year-old son Mark was in from school. I asked him to accompany me to Mr. H's house. His wife was retired, but I was not sure she would be home. "Let all things be done decently and in order," I had learned from my mother and the Bible.

"Come in," Mrs. H stated in reply to my knocking. She cheerfully directed my son and me to some chairs. She knew my mother, so we chatted briefly. Mr. H was seated in a corner. He had spoken when we entered the living room. I said a few casual words, and he responded.

"Mr. H, I came to talk about the Lord Jesus Christ. He has made a tremendous difference in my life. Do you know Him personally?" I asked. Mrs. H. remained pleasant. The expression on her face seemed to have welcomed the conversation.

At this point, Mr. H. spoke in a rough tone of voice. "I am all right! I don't need this! I have been doing just fine!" he said. From this point, every word I said was tossed back at me.

After returning his comments with calm, pleasant words, I said goodbye, as my son Mark and I exited the front door. With a few tears in my eyes, Mark and I made our way home. *You were defeated. You should not have bothered that old man.* It seemed without a shadow of a doubt that the Lord had sent me to witness to Mr. H. about accepting Jesus as his personal Savior.

A few days later, while seated at my work desk, my phone rang. I was used to this. Clients and other workers often called me. I picked up the receiver. "Hamilton County Department of Human Services Child Support Unit, this is Pearlie Forrest speaking. May I help you?" I said.

"This is your mother. Mark has something to tell you," she said. Mother was with Mark after he came home from school. (All my mother's children and grandchildren called her "Mother.") So I waited for Mark to come to the phone.

"Mom! Guess what!" Before I had an opportunity to guess, he continued. "I gave my life to Jesus. I heard what you told Mr. H. the other day. I told Mother that I wanted to give my life to Jesus. I am so happy," Mark said.

There were tears in my eyes again, tears of joy. An old man had rejected the plan of salvation, but my seven year-old son came to know Jesus personally. My witnessing was not in vain. Mark lived a wonderful Christian life through grade school and high school. He graduated at age seventeen and told his pastor and me that he believed the Lord was giving him an assignment to preach His word.

Now, about thirty-plus years later, my son is still preaching and is the pastor of a thriving church. He is also a great singer and skilled musician. His ninety-three year old father, who has a college degree in music, is still skilled on the piano. Sometimes during church worship services, Mark, his father, and his youngest son, thirteen-year-old Mark, Jr., worship with their musical instruments.

Mark is also a great husband to his wife Kelly and a great father to his two sons and daughter. His daughter is now married with a daughter of her own. Who are two of his faithful church members? I am glad you asked! The answer is his father William and I.

My witnessing was about to take a new direction. It would be scary. The agency for which I worked adhered to the law of the "Separation of Church and State." The impulse I felt was kind of fearful. Since I was a Christian, rules and regulations would be obeyed. However, I would not compromise my godly standards. That which lay ahead was surprising. I needed fresh courage.

Chapter 8

THE SKYWALK EXPERIENCE

I had only been employed for a short time when the Lord reminded me that there were people in my department who needed a personal relationship with Him. While I had gained some courage, because of the law of "Separation of Church and State," there remained a bit of apprehension. God reminded me to refrain from sharing my faith on company time. We had a couple of fifteen minute breaks and forty-five minutes for lunch. I believed in giving 100-plus percent on my job. *Share the plan of salvation on a break or lunch time.* I recalled a verse I had memorized from the Bible, "Behold, I stand at the door and knock. If anyone hears My voice and opens the door, I will come in to him and dine with him, and he with Me," Revelation 3:20 (NKJV).

Cearl, one of my coworkers, was a beautiful person. However, she was experiencing some negative personal issues. She was great at interviewing her clients. But in between clients, she complained about unfair situations that she had faced and was facing. I felt an urge from the Holy Spirit to suggest that she and I have lunch together.

"Cearl, let's go to lunch together," I suggested. We chose Roy Rogers. It was a mini restaurant located on Cincinnati's Skywalk. As we sat eating hamburgers and sipping soda pop, I briefly told her about my exciting life with Jesus Christ. She did not respond.

"Do you know Jesus Christ personally?" I asked.

"No! I am not sure that Christianity is for me. There was a church near me, but the members were not friendly. The pastor drove around in expensive cars. He only seemed concerned about himself. So, I stopped going," she said.

I took sips of my soda pop and waited for the Holy Spirit to reveal his response to me.

"I have a suggestion. Do you want to hear it?" I asked.

"Yes," she replied.

"When you give your life to Jesus Christ, you will discover that He is loving and kind and will forever be your Savior and friend. He died on a cruel cross so we may have a fulfilled life on this earth and eternal life in heaven with Him." She didn't respond.

"Romans 3:23 says, 'For all have sinned and come short of the glory God.' At the end of Romans 6:23, there is a wonderful promise. May I continue?"

"Yes," she answered.

"'For the wages of sin is death, but the gift of God is eternal life through Jesus Christ our Lord.' Cearl, will you give your life to Jesus Christ and show the people you have been speaking about, how to love with the love of God? Show them how to live a true Christian life?"

"Yes! Yes!" she said. Tears flowed down her light, brown cheeks. She prayed, "Jesus Christ, I have sinned. Thanks for giving Your life for me. Forgive my sins and come into my life and be my Savior."

Cearl's face glowed. She had been enlightened by God and would become a light in her world. There was joy in our voices as we returned to the far end of the skywalk and took the escalator to Main Street. Upon crossing Main Street, we entered the large office building on Sycamore Street and took our seats at our separate desks.

Cearl and I lived in different parts of Greater Cincinnati, so we decided to meet at work about fifteen minutes early, read a Scripture, and pray together. Our workday began at 8:00 A.M. But, at 7:55 A.M., she returned to her desk to wait for her first client, and I began my paperwork as a clerical worker. We agreed not to use company time for our devotions.

Cearl began sharing her faith as a true follower of Jesus Christ. Once, I saw a co-worker pray to receive Jesus Christ as her personal Savior after Cearl had shared God's Word with her. She was also bold in honoring God. One day, the child support unit had a special meeting with top executives. We were seated around this long conference table. One of the executives began speaking. He used rough profanity. Each time, the phrase began with "God...God... God..." We didn't appreciate his terrible use of words but didn't say anything. Finally, Cearl held up her hand.

"Do you have a question?" the man asked.

"Mister, please don't use God's name like that. He is my Heavenly Father," Cearl said.

"I didn't know that I offended you," the executive said. He never used a curse word again.

There was more work to be done at Hamilton County Department of Human Services Child Support Unit, both naturally and spiritually. Cearl and I were in it for the long haul. My witnessing had only begun. There was a rare awakening waiting.

Chapter 9

TWO IN ONE

A new investigator, I thought as the lady sat a few cubicles down from me and shuffled papers on her desk. I was informed that her name was Lene. She was not a new worker but had returned from sick leave. Lene was quiet, but kind, and smiled when you approached her. Yet, she seemed greatly concerned about something. The clerical supervisor informed me that she was okay, but she and her husband had lost a child. During our break time, I visited her. We introduced ourselves to each other. "How are you?" I asked. She was a little teary-eyed as she revealed some things to me. "Jesus loves you! Do you know Him personally?" I asked.

"No," she answered.

"Would you like to know Him personally by giving your life to Him?" I asked.

"Yes!" she replied.

In her cubicle, she prayed to accept Jesus Christ as her personal Savior. She had done what Romans 10:9-10, and 13 says: "If thou shalt confess with thy mouth, the Lord Jesus, and shalt believe in thine heart that God hath raised Him from the dead, thou shalt be saved. For with the heart, man believeth unto righteousness; and with the mouth, confession is made unto salvation…
..For whosoever shall call upon the name of the Lord shall be saved."

Lene explained that her husband didn't know Jesus personally. I told her that we both would pray for him. "Lene, you can be filled with the Holy Spirit. He gives us power to be overcomers in our daily walk with God. He also gives us a prayer language. It's one that we have not learned. We read about it in Acts chapter two. Christians can praise Him with this gift. Would you like to have this gift?" I asked.

"Yes! I want all that God has for me," she said.

"You can receive this gift in your home. Praise God with 'Hallelujah, Hallelujah…..' until He gives you this beautiful prayer language. Pray in your shower. Until your husband gives his life to God, he might not understand," I said.

She agreed.

A few weeks later, Lene was full of smiles and excitement. "I received my prayer language. It is beautiful and so wonderful," she said. Several months later, she had more wonderful news. Her husband had given his life to the Lord. After faithfully attending church services for a period of time, he told his pastor and Lene that God had called him to preach His word. He prepared for ministry and became a wonderful preacher.

Some time later, I was invited to a birthday dinner. Three minsters sat together. Two of them were Cearl's and Lene's husbands. These ladies were two of the first co-workers I had witnessed to and who had given their lives to Jesus Christ. A scripture comes to mind: "You have not chosen Me, but I have chosen you, that you should go and bring forth fruit, and that your fruit should remain: that whatsoever you shall ask of the Father in My name, He may give it you. These things I command you, that you love one another," John 15:16-17.

As I rejoiced in the Lord, I felt that there was more to come. The beginning of the next phase in my witnessing is kind of humorous now, but it wasn't then. It was no laughing matter.

Chapter 10

CUBICLE INTERRUPTION

One day, I saw my supervisor moving someone into the cubicle next to mine. It was Tula. The idea made me a little unhappy. Tula was a very likeable person. It appeared that the entire department liked her. But she spoke loudly; even her laughter was loud. The previous worker who occupied the cubicle was very soft spoken. However, she had taken another position.

We were allowed to eat lunch at our desks. I usually brought my lunch from home or picked up fruit and a sandwich from the fruit store nearby. Most of my co-workers went out for lunch. It was nice to sit at my desk for the forty-five minutes, eat, and read a favorite book. Tula stayed in for lunch and talked loudly with her friends. *Why Lord? Why the interruption? I enjoy my time with You.* Tula was an investigator, but when she interviewed her clients, she was not loud.

One day, I heard her say over the phone, "I have got to get myself together." *She is beside you for a reason.* It appeared that she had been deeply hurt. Perhaps the loud talking and laughter were a way of coping with her situations.

"Tula, let's go out and have lunch together," I suggested a few days later.

"That's great, Pearlie!" she replied. She was young enough to be my daughter. I found it difficult to reach into her world and make conversation. However, she seemed to have no problem talking to me. We decided on a place where tacos were sold. At the table over lunch, I presented the plan of salvation.

She seemed very anxious. Within a few minutes, she prayed to accept Jesus Christ as her personal Savior.

"You can receive the baptism of the Holy Spirit, speaking in an unlearned language, as it is stated in the Bible in Acts chapter two," I said.

"I want the baptism of the Holy Spirit, too!" she responded. As we walked through alley streets over broken pavements, I prayed for Tula to receive the baptism of the Holy Spirit. She began to praise God. "Hallelujah! Hallelujah! Hallelujah!" Within a few minutes, she was speaking in her heavenly language.

She seemed so excited that I had to calm her down before we got back to work. I didn't want other co-workers to think we had lost our minds.

First Corinthians, chapters 12 and 14 better explain this manner of worshipping God. "He that speaketh in an unknown tongue edifieth himself: but he that prophesies edifieth the church.....I would that you all spake with tongues, but rather that you prophesied: for greater is he that prophesies than he that speaketh with tongues except he interprets, that the church may be edified," I Corinthians 14:4-5.

Jude 1:20 says, "But ye beloved, building up yourselves on your most holy faith, praying in the Holy Ghost." I encourage believers to use this gift in their private devotion, unless their pastor leads them to do otherwise. I praise God daily in my prayer language.

Tula would do great Christian work in witnessing. You will get to know her better in the next chapter. Great excitement propelled me forward!

Chapter 11

ACTION PLEASE

One afternoon, after a long day's work, I relaxed in front of my TV. Within a few minutes I was preparing dinner. There was a knock at my door. I arose and went to answer it. "Who is there?" I asked.

"Tula, Pearlie!" the voice answered. *She just gave her life to Jesus a few days ago. Why is she here?*

As I opened my door, she spoke," Pearlie, this is my friend, Stal. I have been telling her about my recent experience with Jesus Christ. She wants to know Jesus, personally."

After being seated in my living room, I presented the plan of salvation. Stal asked Jesus to forgive her sins, come into her life, and be her Savior. I also informed her how she could receive the baptism of the Holy Spirit. "Yes, I want to receive this experience," she said. Within a few minutes, Stal spoke in a beautiful heavenly language, one she had not learned. We rejoiced together.

A few days later, after work, I was busy with some chores when there was another knock at my door. "Pearlie! This is Tula!" the voice outside the door answered. As I opened the door, I noticed that the lady with her was different than her first friend. "This is my friend, Beth. I also told her about my wonderful experience with Jesus and she wants to have that same experience." The young lady readily asked Jesus to forgive her sins, come into her life, and be her personal Savior. She also received the baptism of the Holy Spirit.

Tula became a living testimony of Jesus Christ among her friends and co-workers. She bubbled with joy. I could tell by her radiant smile. "Pearlie, my friend, Rob, asked me to marry him. I am engaged," she said.

"Does Rob know Jesus personally?" I asked.

"No, but Rob will get saved," she replied.

Carefully and kindly, I cautioned her about marrying an unsaved man. "Why not wait until he gives his life to Jesus," I suggested.

"Rob is going to get saved. I know he will get saved," she stated.

The wedding was planned, and I was invited. My joy was mixed with a little sorrow, as I watched Tula and Rob exchange marriage vows. Each day at work, she was enthusiastic about her marriage and relationship with Jesus Christ. Sometimes, she attended retreats that I organized.

A few months later, Tula was all smiles as she entered my office. We were no longer in cubicles side by side, but we still worked in the same department.

"Pearlie! Rob is here. He wants to give his life to Jesus," she said.

"Where is Rob"? I asked.

"Down in the lobby," she replied.

"Well it is about lunch time. I will take my lunch time and go down and talk with him. Come with me, " I said.

"Oh, no. You go," she suggested.

Our offices were on the fourth floor of the building. So, I took the elevator down to the lobby. Rob was standing near the elevator. "Do you want to accept Jesus Christ, as your personal Savior?" I asked him.

"Yes Madam!" he answered. The lobby was very congested, and I knew he and I could not pray there. So, we walked outside the building. However, it was lunch time for most of those who worked in office buildings in the vicinity of our building, and the sidewalks were crowded. There were also no restaurants nearby.

"Lord, where can we go?" I whispered. Then, I saw the bar across the street that also had eat-in-tables for coffee and limited food. *I don't go to bars! Suppose some of my co-workers see me going in a bar with a young man! What will they think and say? Oh well...*

"Rob, let's go over here and have a cup of coffee," I suggested. There, over coffee, he gave his life to Jesus and wanted to receive the baptism of the Holy

Spirit and his heavenly language. We walked outside the bar, and I noticed a small park nearby. There in the park, Rob received his unlearned heavenly language. He left and went back to his job.

"Tula, Rob gave his life to Jesus and was filled with the Holy Spirit!" I told her.

"Thank you Lord!" she exclaimed as she smiled.

Tula and I continued to work together. Sometimes, on break, we would pray about different situations. She remained a glowing light in her performance and attitude.

However, there was more sharing of God's Word to be done. My excitement grew, only to be tampered, and I mean tampered in a great way!

Chapter 12

Commotion from the Sideline

The pleasant looking lady stood in the doorway of my office and announced, "My name is Bert. I have been selected to escort your client from the first floor waiting room to your office."

"Thank you," I replied.

Whether the client was new or an ongoing case, the referral was given to me in advance. If the client was new, I created a file. An ongoing case file had been located and given to me. I had the necessary forms to do the necessary paperwork as I interviewed the clients.

One day, between clients, I welcomed Bert to sit in my office. During our conversation, I discovered that she did not know Jesus Christ as her personal Savior. "Jesus Christ is a wonderful Savior, and He loves each of us. Have you given your life to Him?" I asked.

"Don't come here with that stuff!" she replied in a harsh voice and quickly left my office. She continued to escort clients to and from my office. I endeavored to be pleasant and kind. But the witnessing with words was set aside.

Bert was on general relief, and her other income was very limited. So one day an idea came to mind. "Bert, may I take you to lunch today?" I asked.

"Yes," she replied as a smile came across her face.

We had a great lunch at a nearby restaurant. The conversation was geared toward what she wanted to talk about.

During my prayer time at home, I prayed for her daily. Later, I learned that she was taking lessons from a religion that didn't believe that Jesus Christ is the divine Son of God.

Several weeks later, during our free time, Bert came to me in tears. Several things had gone wrong in her life. So I listened, without condemning.

"Bert, would you like to give your life to Jesus Christ? He will be your Savior, friend, and meet your every need."

"Yes!" she said, as tears flowed down her cheeks. She prayed to accept Jesus Christ personally.

Over the months and years following, she seemed to enjoy living for Jesus Christ. Later, Bert left this earth. I believe she went to be with God and His Son Jesus Christ. His Holy Spirit gave her the new born-again experience. I remember a Scripture that says: "The Lord is not slack concerning His promise as some men count slackness, but is long suffering, not willing that any should perish, but that all should come to repentance," 2 Peter 3:9.

Muri was a clerical worker and sat near the reception desk. She did her job well, but seemed a little withdrawn. Most of my co-workers and the supervisors knew I enjoyed writing poetry. Sometimes my poems were placed in the agency newspaper that was distributed throughout several departments.

I was chosen "Poet of the Year," and the director had a plaque made in my honor. One day, Muri requested to read one of my booklets. I cheerfully gave it to her but was not prepared for her reply the next day. "I don't agree with anything that you write," she stated as she gave the booklet back to me. I didn't understand, since the booklet had nothing to do with religion or denominations. It was just a book of Christ-centered encouragements. But from that day forward, her attitude toward me changed. However, I treated her with kindness and respect. A verse in Proverbs showed me the way. "He that handles a matter wisely shall find good: and whosoever trusts in the Lord, happy is he," Proverbs 16:20.

I kept writing and allowed those who wanted to read or purchase my books of poetry to do so. My first book entitled, *Knowledge, Wisdom and Laughter*, was self- published. It was mostly about my high school days, family, and friends. Sometimes, I would laugh as I read the poems.

The agency gave me another client escort, Tess. She was intriguing, to say the least, and very kind and diligent at her job. One day, in our spare time, she sat beside my desk and opened a green hardback book that was about two inches thick. "Does your Bible read like this?" she asked as she opened to a certain page.

"Is this your religion?" I asked as I named a certain denomination.

"Yes," she replied.

"I am not changing from who I am," I stated kindly, but firmly.

"Okay! I am not changing, either," she replied.

Tess continued to be a faithful and kind client escort. A short time later, I saw her talking to my co-workers; a few of them I had led to accept Jesus Christ as their personal Savior. *Oh no you don't!* As soon as I got a break, my swift feet took me to each new convert, and they listened. I don't think she was able to get anyone to listen to her.

Christmas was coming up. I knew Tess didn't believe in celebrating Christmas. She was, therefore, omitted from my list of people to give cards or gifts to. When the New Year came around, however, I bought a beautiful umbrella and gave it to Tess. "Thanks! No one ever did this for me," she said. Tess even read one of my books of poems and bought one for her daughter. Several poems were about Jesus.

"My father goes to a Baptist church," she said one day.

"Why don't you accompany him some time?" I suggested.

A few weeks later, she said, "I went with my father to church. It was good.

Christmas is coming up. I will get me a Christmas tree." Her job was soon terminated, and we lost contact with each other. However, I would not be surprised to hear that she gave her life to Jesus Christ.

Sometimes, commotion from the sideline comes from those who are signaling to get into the Christian race. God has all power. A person of a higher status came to mind. But, this seems to be an almost impossibility. Nevertheless, *"With God nothing is impossible!"*

Chapter 13

LITTLE RED LIGHT

Calvin, a videographer, gave me the one-half-inch tape entitled, "Divine Appointment," which he had recorded while I was delivering a message at Truth Temple in Avondale, Ohio. Later, as I popped the tape into my VCR, sat forward on my multi-colored sofa, and watched myself preaching, an idea came to mind. *Teach a Bible Lesson on TV. A great way of witnessing and inviting the unsaved to accept Jesus Christ personally. Another assignment?* I wasn't sure.

For the next several days, the idea turned over several times in my mind. *Should I teach a class? Is this God's will for my life? Can I afford to pay for the air time?* Suddenly, I felt an overwhelming desire to teach on television. With God's direction, it would be possible.

I contacted Calvin. There appeared to be good news. Time Warner cable station would possibly be able to air my program. He said he would only charge fifty dollars for each taping. He also informed me that I would have to call Time Warner and allow them to quote their thirty minute air-time price. This sounded great. I contacted the cable station and was told that air-time, for non-profit organizations was free to those who qualified. *What if I don't qualify?* I brushed the question aside and moved forward.

On that chilly October day, as I headed to the television station, I was a little apprehensive. *Negative thoughts will not stop me now!* Inside the station, I was fascinated with the different sets. They were designed with thick paneled walls on three sides and the fourth wall was enclosed with thick glass.

I carefully completed the application given to me. A great feeling of relief soothed my mind when the director approved my application. The instructor made a presentation regarding the requirements for the program. "If the requirements are not met, we will pull your tape while your program is in progress and inform you. If this continues, we will cancel your program," she said.

We were instructed on how to operate the cameras. When the little red button comes on, it's time for you to begin your presentation. She dwelt on the little red button. *The little red button! The little red button!* This stuck in my mind. Some of the most tedious features were focusing and refocusing the lenses by zooming in and out. *Lord, I really need your help!*

The cameras could be borrowed and taken off the premises. Programming could be done at home or at another location of our own choosing. We were then taken to the editing room and given instructions. We had to edit our own tapes. A three-quarter-inch tape was required for each program. I decided not to borrow their camera. My son Mark had a camcorder and promised to do the taping, but it would have to be taken to a production company and transferred to three-quarter-inch tapes.

Mark and his family lived in Columbus, Ohio, more than 200 miles round trip. Nevertheless, he came down to do my first taping. That first taping will forever be stamped in my memory. My makeshift set took place in my dining room. A large stand filled with running vines served as a backdrop. Seated at a small desk with my Bible and notes, I rehearsed Psalms 8:1, "O Lord, our Lord, how excellent is Your Name in all the earth." This was followed by introducing myself. "Hi! My name is Pearlie Forrest. God loves you right where you are."

My television program was entitled, *Pearlie Forrest Presents*. At the beginning of the program, the title was displayed while fifteen seconds of music played. I was thrilled as Mark pointed the "Little Red Light" towards me, but I froze, to say the least. All I could hear in my mind, over and over, was *Little Red Light! Little Red Light!*

"Cut!" Mark said. Then he continued, "Mom don't just look at the little red light. Begin speaking. Your audience is behind the little red light. Envision them."

Suddenly! *A family in their living room. A mother watching TV while cooking.* I felt God's presence while speaking. About twenty-five minutes later, I gave the invitation for someone to accept Jesus as their personal Savior. "Do you know Jesus Christ personally? Have you ever asked Him to forgive your sins, come into your life, and be your Savior?" Romans 3:23 says, "For all have sinned and come short of the glory of God." Romans 6:23 says, "The wages of sin is death: but the gift of God is eternal life through Jesus Christ our Lord." I concluded with, "If you would like to pray with me, please repeat the follow-ing: 'Lord, Jesus, I have sinned. Please forgive my sins and come into my life and be my Savior." I then gave an address where they could write to me. Finally, the theme music played, and I promised to be back the following week.

By the time Mark left, we had just finished my first twenty-eight-minute telecast. I found a company a few miles from my home, where I had the eight-millimeter tape transferred to a three-quarter-inch tape. At Time Warner, I presented the three-quarter-inch tape. My twenty-eight-minute program would be aired in the evening twice a week, which made it possible to be home from work before my program began.

There was joy in each step. "Lord, thank you!" I said. My mind took me back to one of the first television programs I remembered. The name of the series was *Wagon Train*. "It is time for *Wagon Train*," someone would say, and we would gather around the TV. The theme music was played and then pic-tures of the main stars appeared in motion. I looked at the clock and whispered, "It's almost time for *Pearlie Forrest Presents*." At home alone? No really. I began to reminiscence.

Several years ago when I gave my life to Jesus Christ, He showed me a large screen, though in the spirit, it seemed so real. The scenery was almost breathtaking. I saw the gorgeous river that had washed my sins away. On the side where I now stood, the grass was green and manicured. The flowers were amazingly beautiful. Oh, the joy that flooded my soul. Perhaps God was giving me a glimpse of having my own TV program. O, it can never be as beautiful as His world, but it is beautiful, nevertheless.

"Oh it's time! It's time!" I shouted. My family and some friends had been notified of the air time. I was reluctant to tell a lot of people. Negative criticism has a way of weighing one down. A previous program ended. There was station identification. Then my theme music was heard loud and clear. Unfolding before my tearful, joyful eyes was *Pearlie Forrest Presents*. I appeared on the TV screen with, "O Lord, our Lord, how excellent is Thy Name in all the earth. God loves you right where you are..."

Have you ever watched one of those touching movies and cried through every scene? I think I cried through my entire program. "Was it that bad?" you ask. No! It was wonderful, if I do say so myself! God helps us to do what may seem impossible. He is the Almighty God.

Towards the end of the program, doubt tried to creep in. *I gave my address and will probably receive a lot of criticism. Now, what will I do? How will my critics be answered? What if Time Warner cancels my program? It will be very embarrassing.*

Suddenly my thoughts changed. *God is with me. He will see me through. I trust and obey Him and ask for the guidance of His Holy Spirit. He promised never to leave me nor forsake me.* I would encourage others with God's Word.

Looking ahead, there seemed to be many more of God's promises. So, I began studying for the upcoming programs, while working in my church. Witnessing primarily to young people, there was a particular situation with two young sisters about ten and twelve years of age. They were placed in my Bible class.

I knew that using flannel graft on TV might not be feasible, but in a church Bible study with children, it seemed appropriate. I used different colors as I presented the plan of salvation. Red represented the blood of Jesus. "Jesus was badly beaten and nailed to a cruel cross. He died for our sins, was buried, and arose the third day. A few weeks later, He went back to heaven to prepare a beautiful place for us. All those who ask Jesus to forgive their sins, come into their lives, and be their Savior will go to live with Him." This was the essence of my message.

The two sisters raised their hands at the same time. Their parents were not there. In fact, their parents were members of another church. "Would you like to give your life to Jesus Christ?" I asked.

"Yes! Yes!" they replied. I asked a few more questions to determine if they had heard me clearly and if it was really their desire to know Jesus Christ personally. Each prayed to receive Jesus Christ personally. There were several children in the class, but no one mocked them. Neither did they agree to give their lives to Jesus.

Being children at their ages, did it last? They accompanied their parents to church, but I never heard of them being disobedient children. I heard that these girls' parents later gave their lives to the Lord. The youngest girl grew up and got married. Today, her husband is a pastor, and she works with him.

As I prepared for my telecasts, I continued witnessing one-on-one. Sometimes I worked with CURE (Christians United Reaching Everyone). Most of the people we witnessed to were from the slum areas and had never been to a church service. Thank God for the opportunities!

I continued doing my weekly TV programs, but there was about to be a great change. *Doing the impossible?* It appeared that way. So, my prayer time increased. I needed to talk to God a lot. He has all knowledge and all wisdom.

Chapter 14

MULTIMEDIA PRIVILEGES

I was enjoying my weekly television program, but it was causing Mark and his family a lot of time on their off days to travel 200 miles round trip to tape my programs. "Be considerate of others," I whispered. "What should I do, Lord?"

"Do your own taping. Walk in on the set," He replied.

"But I need a camera. I don't want to borrow Time Warner's camera."

A few days later, I went to the television station to pick up my tape which had been aired. There beside my large three-quarter-inch tape laid a one-half-inch tape. It appeared that these tapes were suitable for airing. If I was permitted to use the one-half-inch tape, the high cost of transferring from eight millimeter to three-quarter-inch tape would be eliminated.

"May I use the one-half-inch tape for my programs?" I asked the director.

"Yes," he answered.

I asked Mark to come down and take me to an electronic store. The Lord had given me the money to purchase a large camera and tripod. Mark showed me some features, taped a program, and left. A few days later, it was time to do another taping. I remembered God's voice. "Walk in on the set." I prepared for taping by setting the camera on the tripod in front of my desk. The recorded tape with pre-recorded music was placed near. Notes for my teaching had been prepared and placed on my desk.

As the theme music played, I turned on the camera and began speaking. "O Lord, our Lord, how excellent is Thy name in all the earth." At this moment, I appeared on the screen and continued. "Hi! My name is Pearlie Forrest. God loves you right where you are." My teaching began and closed with an opportunity for those who had not accepted Jesus as personal Savior to do so.

Weekly telecasts with my teaching were going fine. However, I also like to write poetry. I discovered that Time Warner had an educational channel. "Will you air videos of my poetry reading on your educational channel?" I asked. I was given a twenty-eight-minute time slot that aired once a week. The poetry writing was usually done in an outside setting. Some videos took place on my street, which was heavily lined with trees. Others took place beside streams of water. One of the most beautiful videos had a large lake with ducks as a backdrop.

A lot of the young people and schools had programs on the educational channel. Some of my poems talked about God and His universe. Even though this station was owned by Time Warner, I guess the directors didn't like the God part, which was another way of witnessing, because they cancelled my program. However, I was allowed to continue teaching the Bible and reading poetry on the main station, which still aired twice a week.

I attended church at least twice each week and was an altar worker, along with my sister Ethel Pearl. When someone answered the altar call my pastor made and wanted to accept Jesus as personal Savior or be filled with the Holy Spirit, Pastor Smith called my sister and me to the altar. We took them into the Prayer Room. Many gave their lives to the Lord and received their "prayer language" through the gift of the Holy Spirit.

Sometimes, during praise and worship services, I was seated next to a person who hadn't confessed Jesus as their personal Savior. I felt led of the Lord, to whisper to them, "Would you like to accept Jesus as your Savior?"

They often whispered, "Yes." I would quietly lead them in prayer and watched as tears flowed from their eyes. Others, with radiant smiles, said, "Lord Jesus, forgive my sins. Come into my life and be my Savior!"

There were times when I led them into receiving the baptism of the Holy Spirit, speaking in their heavenly language. The praise and worship services were never disturbed. However, once, I was a little embarrassed. Mrs. Harvey, who lived in another state, knew the Lord personally. One day, on a visit to her son, she said, "The next time I come to Cincinnati, I want you to lead me into receiving the baptism of the Holy Spirit."

One night, during a worship service at my church, I noticed that she was seated behind me. I quietly went to her and said, "Praise the Lord by saying 'Hallelujah! Hallelujah! Hallelujah!'" This was usually the way I led people into receiving the Holy Spirit with their prayer language. Praising God would cause them to take their minds off of everything and focus only on God.

Mrs. Harvey smiled and said, "I received the baptism of the Holy Spirit a few weeks ago." I had to laugh at myself. Well, I was told to "Knock on Every Door," or use every available opportunity. So, I got a little carried away.

Let's go on with the multimedia. I had taken some journalism courses at the University of Cincinnati because I wanted to be a reporter. However, my mother's illness, my care for her, my job, and the children prevented me from getting a degree. I don't regret it. It was a privilege to take care of my mother.

As you have guessed, I enjoy writing. Therefore, in addition to my weekly television program, I decided to do a monthly correspondence by mail. The first booklet, *Involved*, which usually consisted of sixteen pages, was mailed to several people. Many responded in a positive way.

My television ministry was still growing. I was surprised one day when one of my co-workers Diane Mingo, who was always quiet, stopped me near my desk to commend me. "Pearlie, I saw you on television last night. You didn't tell me that you have a television program. It was great!" My son Mark and her son David were in their preteens at the time. Years later, she said, "Pearlie, you were a great inspiration to me. You helped me a lot." Even though we are now older with adult grandchildren, we still correspond often. Today, Diane is a wonderful Christian woman whose conversations are always about the Lord.

One day I decided to go to Fountain Square in Downtown Cincinnati to do some witnessing. There was always a crowd there eating sack lunches from a nearby restaurant or just talking and watching the water flow. I saw a lady standing by herself. "This is a good opportunity," I thought silently.

"Miss, do you know Jesus personally?" I asked as kindly as I knew how. That lady took off, as if I had drawn a gun on her. It appeared that "My Assignment" had backfired. Oh, well, I knew that I could not and would not neglect "My Assignment." More opportunities would come my way, and I would continue to tell others about the wonderful and unconditional love of Jesus Christ.

My weekly television programs lasted for four years, from October 1994 until October 1998. In September 1998, I retired from my position as an investigator for the Child Support Unit of the Hamilton County Department of Human Services in Cincinnati, Ohio. By October, and I only had a couple of weeks before I would move out of state. I reflected on some that I had witnessed to and never seen again.

Fleeting Moments

1. Four ladies had come to my house. They prayed to receive Jesus as their personal Savior. However, I didn't get their telephone numbers or addresses and never saw them again.
2. I prayed for a lady in a hospital. She passed away a short time later, before I got a chance to see her again.
3. Ronnie was in the Hamilton detention center. His aunt, a co-worker of mine, asked me to visit him. I witnessed of God's love and power through the little open slots in the glass window. He listened attentively and prayed to accept Jesus as his personal Savior. I never saw him again. However, his aunt says he became a changed man, and when he got out of prison, his lifestyle was different.
4. Late one night, I was called to a home. The lady had told her mother that she wanted to give her life to Jesus. My sister Ethel and I prayed for her to accept Jesus personally and be filled with the Holy Spirit. However, I have not seen her since.

When my two weeks of living in Cincinnati were up, I packed my furniture in a U-Haul truck. My son-in-law Freddie and his brother Connie drove it about

700 miles to my new location in Collins, Georgia. I came a few days later. Collins, my hometown, is located approximately sixty miles west of Savannah, Georgia. *Would I be able to continue "My Assignment" as usual?* I prayed I would.

Chapter 15

BEYOND BOUNDARIES

Witness to my supervisor? What if she becomes offended and gives me a bad evaluation? What if she shrewdly increases my caseload? These are some of the questions that pressed deeply upon my mind. However, my passion for my divine assignment continued and would not go away.

My supervisor Nan was a great supervisor and gave me top evaluations. She consulted Mr. J., the director, and got his approval to allow me to serve as supervisor of the unit while she was on maternity leave. A few months later, Nan returned to her position. But a short time later she resigned so she could be a stay-at-home mom. Her husband had become an attorney.

While I had no desire to become a supervisor, the urge to witness to Nan was on my mind. As I entered Nan's office, she asked me to take a seat. There, I presented the plan of salvation. "Jesus, forgive my sins, come into my life, and be my Savior," she prayed. I didn't see Nan again. However, her husband would stop by my office and give me messages from her. It appeared she was enjoying her life with Jesus Christ.

Kela became supervisor of our unit. She was fair, but very strict. Some days, I had up to ten clients. Sometimes, it would take an hour to do a particular client. This was followed by an abundance of paperwork. Packets had to be done for court cases. Some days were very stressful, but God saw me through.

Kela was young but discovered that her health was rapidly deteriorating. From our casual conversations, I discovered that she didn't know Jesus Christ personally. Her mother was a devout Christian. However, it appeared that Kela didn't want any of her mother's "religion." I had an overwhelming desire to witness to Kela, even though I was a little apprehensive. "Kela, would you like to take a mid-morning break?" I asked as I entered her office.

"Okay!" she replied.

We walked up the stairs to the cafeteria, got snacks, and sat at a vacant table. "I have something that I sincerely believe God wants me to say to you," I said.

"What is it?" she asked.

I presented the plan of salvation. With tears streaming down her face, she asked Jesus to forgive her sins, come into her life, and be her Savior. By this time, our break was over. I suggested that she tell her mother about her new experience with Jesus. A few days later, I asked if she had told her mother. "No!" she responded.

Later, I discovered Kela had joined a religion that didn't believe in Jesus Christ but only the Old Testament. She was still a good supervisor and gave me great evaluations but never mentioned the name of Jesus. Some time later, she requested that I receive a large bonus.

Later, a minister became a part of our unit. He witnessed to Kela. I was told that she really accepted Jesus personally and had gone to be with Him. There were more "worlds to conquer" that would involve not adhering to the rules of "The Separation of Church and State."

Chapter 16

CHANNELED TO THE TOP

The agency for which I worked was having financial problems. There were several departments that began to downsize. Several supervisors had to take lower positions. Once promised wage increases were now frozen. An outside agency requested to take part of our caseload. They promised to do a better job. Even though we had protested earlier in a professional way, the outside agency was hired.

Call the people to prayer. Pray on the sixteenth floor. Is this the Lord speaking to me or my own intuition? I tried to set the thought aside, but it was there during the workday and after I arrived home. *Call the people to pray* occupied my mind.

"OK!" But I still procrastinated.

Our salaries came from the state and federal government. Although it was a "Separation of Church and State" situation, no one complained about me sharing my experience with Jesus Christ with co-workers and supervisors because "company time" was not used. *However, public prayer is different. Or is it? I can't ignore God's command.* This question was impressed upon my mind.

"Pearlie, the Lord said for you to call us to prayer on the 16th floor," Tula stated as she passed me in the hallway. I did not respond at the time, but thought, *How does she know what God told me?* I had told absolutely no one, inside or outside the agency. At this time, our department was on the third floor. The sixteenth floor was reserved for meetings called by the director, attorneys, and college and university professors. I had even taken college courses up there.

Between the first and sixteenth floors there were several administrations, including the county courts: Domestic Relations, Common Pleas, Juvenile, and others. The County Probation Department occupied an entire floor. Several attorneys had their offices on particular floors. Department of Human Services Caseworkers and Children Services occupied several floors. There were other county businesses as well. *If a group of employees and I pray on the sixteenth floor, we will be over all of these people. Will they like this?* I would have to go through several channels to get permission to reserve the sixteenth floor on a specific date and time. A carefully worded memo, with a specific date during "Lunch Hour Time" requesting permission was typed and given to my immediate supervisor. She promised to pass it to her supervisor. The memo had to travel to the director. If he granted the permission, the memo would be given to security and those who scheduled different activities. In the meantime, I gave the situation to God.

A few days later, I received a memo stating that my request had been granted. "Thank You Father God!" I whispered. I typed a memo to all of my co-workers and others in the agency. Many met with me on the sixteenth floor on that chosen day and time. We held hands and prayed. Tears flowed down most of our faces as we asked God to help administration come up with a plan that would be beneficial to all involved.

A few days later, I asked permission to pray on the sixteenth floor again. The request was granted. A short time later, the downsizing ceased. Not only was the freeze taken off of our wages, but we received bonuses.

I continued telling others, employees and clients, about the love of God. One day I went to the waiting room and escorted a client to my office. She was very cooperative and kind and signed all the required documents. I prepared to escort her back to the waiting room for exit. However, she remained seated and appeared very sad. There was some time before my next scheduled client. So, I sat back down. "Is there something wrong?" I asked. In tears, she began to tell me of her adverse situations. Life had not been too kind to her. Bad situations had overwhelmed her. "Jesus loves you! He is your answer! Do you know Him personally?" I asked.

"No," she replied.

"Would you like to know Him personally?" I asked.

"Yes," she replied. She repeated the prayer and invited Jesus into her life to be her personal Savior. As she raised her head, a smile was on her face. She said "Thank you" as I escorted her to the waiting room.

There was an employee in the agency, not necessarily a co-worker, that I felt the Lord leading me to. She greatly amazed me. I am sure she will astonish you also.

Chapter 17

MISS INTAKE

Miss Intake is a name I gave a worker in the department who interviewed clients for different parts of the agency. Her cubicle was near the entrance to my department. Whenever I passed her desk, she had a radiant smile. However, Miss Intake was legally blind, so she had had difficulty getting the position.

The agency employed handicapped people, but most of them were typists who gathered their information from recordings or live voices. Miss Intake had to read and familiarize herself with several forms. She had to read the information to the clients and have them sign the forms. She pleaded with personnel to allow her to take the position and said she would memorize the forms. They put her on probation for a few months. Co-workers helped her memorize several different forms. She was able to read the headings and see the signature lines. Her supervisor evaluated her and witnessed her dedication, great typing, and public relations skills.

Miss Intake became an excellent interviewer, surpassing some of her co-workers who had twenty-twenty vision. She obeyed the rules of the agency, and clients didn't become offended when she could not grant all of their desires. They respected her because she respected them.

When I heard about this outstanding young woman, I wanted to interview her for my monthly publication, *Involved*, which was later entitled *The Inspirational*. One day during our break, Miss Intake agreed to an interview. We talked a few minutes as I asked her about her hobbies. "People!" People were her hobby. She loved people and enjoyed interviewing them and conversing with her co-workers during lunch and breaks. She didn't complain but told me how she had lost most of her vision. The retina had been destroyed by a disease. Her optometrist said her eyesight could never be restored and that she would finally lose complete vision in both eyes.

"Do you know Jesus personally? Have you ever asked Him to forgive your sins, come into your life, and be your personal Savior?" I asked calmly.

"No. I go to church but have never asked Him to be my personal Savior," she replied. After reciting a few scriptures, she prayed to accept Jesus personally.

"Regarding your eyes, God still works miracles," I said.

Some time later, when the next issue of my monthly publication came out, I brought her a copy and read her the interview we had done.

"I believe my sight will be restored! I will not need this white cane to help me find bumps and uneven pavements," she said.

In the afternoons while I left work, I would see Miss Intake with her white cane crossing the street and making it to the bus stop. I didn't talk much with her. There was another and more convenient entrance/exit to my department, and the staff was advised to use it.

A few months later, I couldn't believe my eyes. Miss Intake made her way across the street with no cane. I was informed by a close friend that she no longer needed her white cane. Her eyesight was being restored. Some time later, Miss Intake was awarded a nice house, debt free! After a few minor repairs, she moved into her beautiful home.

"Delight thyself also in the Lord; and He shall give you, the desires of thine heart," Psalms 37:4. I couldn't help but to consider just how amazing God is, as more contacts were waiting.

Chapter 18

AMAZING CONTACTS

Each afternoon after working with my clients at the Department of Human Services, I would go home and cook dinner. My son Mark enjoyed the meal with me. After dinner, he did his homework. Sometimes, I assisted him before reading and typing articles. Each month I produced a daily devotional entitled *Involved* that was distributed locally and mailed to subscribers in different states.

One evening at about 7:00 P.M. there was a knock on my door. As I opened the door, Jenny, a close friend, stood there with a couple of young ladies.

"These are my friends and I told them about your desire to lead people to the Lord. They want to get saved and be filled with the Holy Spirit," she said. The ladies were eager and prayed to receive Jesus Christ as their personal Savior. A few minutes later, they asked Jesus to fill them with the Holy Spirit. Almost immediately they began to speak in their heavenly languages. It was a language they had not learned because all of us only spoke English. They were overwhelmed with joy and praised God.

A few days later, Jenny brought three other ladies to my house.

"These are friends and co-workers of mine. They want to be saved and filled with the Holy Spirit," she said. All three ladies asked Jesus to forgive their sins, come into their lives, and be their Savior. Two of the ladies asked Jesus to fill them with His Holy Spirit. Within about five to six minutes they began to speak in their heavenly languages. The third lady, who had remained quiet while the others received this joyful experience, had an astonished look on her face.

"I need some more information. Is this necessary?" she asked.

"May I read about the first group in the Bible that spoke in their heavenly language on the day of Pentecost?" I asked.

"Yes! Of course!" she replied.

I began reading Acts chapter two, verse one: "When the day of Pentecost was fully come, they were all with one accord in one place. And suddenly there came a sound from heaven as of a rushing mighty wind, and it filled the house where they were sitting. And there appeared unto them cloven tongues like as of fire, and sat upon each of them. And they were all filled with the Holy Spirit, and began to speak with other tongues, as the Spirit gave them..."

The lady interrupted me. "I am ready! I am ready! Praise God!" Within a minute, she began speaking in her beautiful heavenly language.

"I have never known a foreign language. Now, I praise God with a gift He has given me," she said.

I believe the gift of speaking in tongues is given for our own daily devotion. We must allow the Holy Spirit to use us each day. However, I believe there are times when He will allow the pastors to permit this gift to be manifested in their churches or worship services. Unless He does so, we should remain silent. "Let all things be done decently and in order," 1 Corinthians 14:40. "He that speaketh in an unknown tongue speaketh not unto men, but unto God; for no man understandeth him; however, in the Spirit, he speaketh mysteries." 1 Corinthians 14:2.

On another occasion, my sister Geraldine brought a couple of friends to my house. They received Jesus as their personal Savior and were filled with the baptism of the Holy Spirit. These ladies left full of joy.

One Sunday, my brother Hosea, his wife Polly, and their five teenage girls came from Detroit to Cincinnati. They visited our church and later came to our house. After dinner, the Holy Spirit prompted me to ask, "How many of you young people want to be saved and filled with the Holy Spirit?" Two of them readily accepted Jesus as their personal Savior and were filled with the Holy Spirit.

My next-door neighbors James (Butch) and Helen were nice. However, I came to realize that they didn't know Jesus Christ personally. It wasn't just because they didn't attend church, but their lifestyles didn't reflect Jesus Christ.

I had planned to invite them to my church worship service. After a few years, I still had not gotten around to it. Procrastination kept getting in my way.

I was soon informed that James was in the hospital. He was a young man with terminal cancer and a short time to live. My sister Ethel Pearl took me to see him. As we stood by his bed, we could see that he was in severe pain. but he talked to us in a whisper.

"Butch, would you like to know Jesus Christ personally?" I asked.

"Yes," he whispered. I quoted a few scriptures and asked him to repeat a prayer. "Jesus, forgive my sins, come into my heart, and be my Savior."

"Where is Jesus?" I asked.

"In my heart," Butch replied. Ethel and I didn't stay long. But, as we were walking away from his bed toward the door, we heard him whisper, "He is in my heart! Jesus is in my heart!"

A short time later he passed from this life into eternity. I was away on vacation for a few days, but when I returned I contacted Helen. She spoke of an observation she had as Butch was passing out of this life. "I don't understand. Butch was smiling as he was passing. Later, as I observed him at the funeral home, he still had a great smile on his face."

"Helen, Butch accepted Jesus as his personal Savior. Would you like to know Jesus personally?" I asked.

"Yes," she replied. There over the phone she recited the prayer to accept Jesus Christ personally. I also led her into receiving the baptism of the Holy Spirit. I could hear her praising the Lord and speaking in her heavenly language, a language she had not learned.

Praise God! He is wonderful! There was more to come, but I needed to "put on my traveling shoes."

Chapter 19

TRAVELING SHOES

My nephew Caesar Romero, or Butch, as his family called him, lived with his parents Alvin and Beatrice in Miami, Florida. Alvin was my oldest brother. Butch was now in his mid-thirties. When he was a child and throughout his teens he accompanied his parents and nine siblings to church services. His parents were devout Christians and ministers.

Butch became a skilled musician on the saxophone. After high school, he enrolled in college but later dropped out and began to play with a professional band. He stopped going to church and lived an ungodly lifestyle. He eventually developed a severe disease. Doctors said there was no cure and he was in the last stage of this illness. His parents talked to him about giving his life to the Lord, but he procrastinated. I suppose he thought he would get better.

It was mid-December, but I had an overwhelming desire to go to Miami and talk to Butch. Ice and snow were all over Cincinnati. Most days the temperature was at zero or below. However, I was reminded that God loves all people. The scripture says, "The Lord is not slack concerning His promise, as some men count slackness; but is longsuffering to us-ward, not willing that any should perish, but that all should come to repentance," 2 Peter 3:9.

My job granted my two-weeks-vacation request. I would have to make the over 2,500 mile round-trip by bus to Miami, Florida. It was icy, but I took a taxicab the fifteen miles from my home to the Greyhound bus station in downtown Cincinnati. It was no fun sliding all the way, but I didn't have a choice.

It was good to be on a nice bus. We crossed the Ohio River, which was covered with ice. Interstate-75 was fairly clear. We stopped in Lexington, Kentucky and picked up some more passengers. I reclined my seat and took a nap but suddenly awoke and wondered why the bus was traveling so slowly. Peering out the window, I saw a frightening sight. Cars in each direction, East and West-bound, were sliding off the pavement into the median. Interstate-75 was a solid sheet of ice! I began to pray for my safety and the safety of others. "God is our refuge and strength, a very present help in trouble," Psalms 46:1.

About twenty-four hours later, the bus arrived in Miami. Later, relaxing in my brother and sister-in-law's home, I heard a noise. At the window, I could not believe my eyes. A man nearby was mowing a lawn. It was eighty degrees. In Cincinnati, lawnmowers had been stored away since late September.

Alvin and Beatrice worked. Eight of their ten children were at their own homes. The youngest, Francine, was in college. During the day, Butch just laid around. He was very sick. I mostly read. Then came the urge to talk to him about the Lord. He listened attentively and said he wanted to give his life to the Lord. Butch prayed to accept Jesus Christ personally and be filled with the Holy Spirit. My mission was accomplished. "It is God which worketh in you, both to will and do of His good pleasure," Philippians 2:13.

A short time later, Butch passed away, but not before leaving a great testimony. He had asked God to forgive him, but he also asked his parents to forgive him. He said, "I am going to be with Jesus!" A few months later, my "travel" would take a different direction.

Chapter 20

FOR THIS PURPOSE

I sensed that the Lord was sending me in another direction. *Where? What is the assignment?* My job received my uttermost attention, so I busied myself interviewing clients.

Oh no! I forgot this bill. It has mounted up to $139 and must be paid to Berean Bookstore within one week. I had just gotten paid and only had carfare plus about twenty dollars left. My next pay period was two weeks away. However, the bill had to be paid because it was not my practice to be late for anything, especially financial situations.

Seed faith. Plant a seed and allow God to honor it. Now where did that come from? Suddenly, I remembered correspondence from Oral Roberts. I had been receiving His encouraging letters once a month for the past several years. However, I would only send him about five dollars with a response twice a year. My donation total for the past several years had amounted to less than fifty dollars. I then remembered that it was Monday, June 15, 1976, and the payment of $139 was due the following Monday, June 22, 1976.

I found Evangelist Oral Roberts' address in my purse and sent him twenty dollars, which was not very much money in 1976, but it was all I had. My family and I were close, but I didn't inform anyone of the debt or the money I had sent to Evangelist Roberts.

Friday, June 19 was my birthday. No one had planned anything to my knowledge. It was Bible study night, and my pastor always taught. My sister Ethel picked me up and took me to church. There were a lot of cars parked nearby. *There are a lot of people at Bible study. More than usual. Oh well.*

"Happy birthday!" Voices rang out as I walked through the church door. Many people were there, including an attorney who handled my court cases. It was a great surprise my sister Ethel had planned.

I received many gifts. When I got home, I counted the money. "$139. And there is more and many other gifts," I whispered.

Approximately seven months later, I received a letter from Evangelist Roberts. It read, "You are invited to our 1977 Spring Seminar. You are invited for the four days and three nights of classes and meetings. If you are taking public transportation, you will only need your fare to and from Tulsa, Oklahoma. Your hotel room, food, and transportation to and from your hotel will be provided. Give us your arrival date, time, and place of arrival and one of our courtesy cars will pick you up and bring you to Mabley Center on the Oral Roberts University campus."

The request for vacation time from my job was granted. I informed the ORU Committee that I would arrive in Tulsa, Oklahoma on Thursday at 5:00 A.M. On Wednesday at noon I boarded the Greyhound bus, and upon my arrival to the bus station in Tulsa, a young student from ORU put my luggage in his car and took me to Mabley Center.

Hundreds were present at the center. Some were even half asleep as we waited for further instructions. I tried to get some shut-eye myself, but a lady nearby carried on with non-stop laughter and talking. Her friends, or those with her, couldn't get a word in edgewise.

One of the student hosts spoke softly to me and asked, "Is it all right if you have a roommate?"

"Yes," I replied. *I sure hope it is not that lady that is running her mouth nonstop. How can it be? There are several hundred people here.*

At about 11:00 A.M. a shuttle bus took us to different hotels. I heard that ORU had reserved space in eight different hotels. Walking into the lobby of the hotel where I would be staying for the next three nights, I noticed that there were about fifty of us. Luggage was everywhere. A hostess told me that my room would be ready in about an hour as she gave us a slip of paper with the room number 121.

It was about 12:00 P.M., and we would not to be back to Mabley Center until 5:00 P.M., so there was time to shower and take a long nap before service. Sitting there in the hotel lobby, I heard laughter and steady talking. *It's her! There she is, again! Oh well, I don't have to share a room with her.*

"What room are you in?" someone asked her.

"Room 121," she replied.

I almost fell off my seat. Tears wanted to fall from my weary, sleepy eyes. *Get control of yourself.* We introduced ourselves, I learned her name was Connie, and we made our way to Room 121 where we began unpacking. Connie continued to talk. "Let me shut up and let you get some rest," she said.

After a great time of relaxation, she and I dressed and went to Mabley Center. I discovered that there were about 2,000 people in attendance for the seminar.

The next day after breakfast, the morning class began at 10:00 A.M. President Roberts stated that several people wanted to receive the baptism of the Holy Spirit. They were to remain after dismissal, and his own selected workers would lead them into receiving the Holy Spirit. "I will stay. This is one reason that I came to the seminar, to receive the baptism of the Holy Spirit," Connie said.

"I will take the shuttle back to our hotel," I replied.

About an hour later, Connie returned to the hotel room looking sad. "What's wrong? Are you all right?" I asked her.

"I am disappointed. They prayed for me, but the gift of tongues, my heavenly language, never came forth." *For this purpose, you are here. Pray with her. She will receive her heavenly language."* I prayed with Connie, and within a few minutes, she spoke in a beautiful language that she had not learned. There were tears of joy!

Connie and I became best friends, even though she lived in Sycamore Illinois, and I in Cincinnati, Ohio, she was a great inspiration to me. We corresponded for about thirty-five years. Since she was much older, her health eventually began to fail, and we lost contact with each other.

The entire seminar was great. Sunday came, an ORU student took me back to the Greyhound bus station, and I made my way home. I learned several things from the conference. Some of the greatest were: (1) God uses whomever He will (2) Don't get caught up with my own selfish desires allowing the annoyance of small things to interfere with God's plans, and (3) Always be ready to give God the glory and honor. I also came to realize that summer vacations can become overwhelming when they include God's plans. Exploring the beach and discovering different parts of the world can be exotic, but discovering God's precious gems is most amazing, especially in one's hometown.

Chapter 21

THE ROAD LEADS ONWARD

After retiring from Hamilton County and moving back to my hometown of Collins, Georgia, I lived with my daughter Annette, her husband Freddie, and their five teenage children. It was wonderful. I joined a local church and became active. However, my desire was to do some door-to-door witnessing. Annette and Freddie lived in a farming area approximately three miles from town, and I didn't drive. I also had severe back problems. Therefore, it was difficult to walk at least two miles to the outskirts of town and three miles into the city.

Early evenings, after Annette and Freddie returned from work, sometimes they had visitors. Some of these visitors came for prayer to receive Jesus personally or to be filled with the Holy Spirit and their prayer language. One might ask if the prayer language is beneficial. Yes! It is an encourager to you as an individual. "He that speaks in an unknown tongue edifies himself..." I Corinthians 14:4. Jude, verse 20, also says, "Ye beloved, building up yourselves in your most holy faith, praying in the Holy Ghost."

Tongues can also be beneficial to others, if someone has the spiritual gift of interpretation. "Wherefore let him that speaks in an unknown tongue, pray that he may interpret." If you are in church, always get permission from the pastor before you use your prayer language. I usually pray each day in tongues during my private devotion. This helps to build me up spiritually. I love to praise God in this manner.

After I purchased my own home in Collins a year later, some people came to my house. As I witnessed to the unsaved, they saw their need for Jesus and prayed to receive Him personally. Some received the Holy Spirit and spoke in unknown tongues.

In time, God healed my back, and I was able to walk the one to two miles to a more populated area on the outskirts of Collins, since I lived a little closer than Annette and Freddie. I even became involved in child care and led one of the mothers to the Lord. "Knock on every door." The echo was loud and clear.

Later, I took a part-time job with Tattnall County's afterschool enrichment program, where I tutored at-risk students. I witnessed to some of my students, and they accepted Jesus as their personal Savior. One of my co-workers, a tutor, prayed to accept Jesus. An instructor from another school also received the Holy Spirit and her prayer language.

More souls continued being added to the body of Christ. Two store owners, two of my former classmates, a mechanic, and a construction worker all prayed to receive Jesus as their personal Savior. The occupation or background didn't matter. It seemed that many were hungry for a relationship with Jesus Christ.

A seventy-plus year-old lady who became a member of a church when she was in her early teens listened to me as I witnessed to her. Having known her since I was a child, there was no evidence that she knew Jesus personally. She stated that she had never asked Jesus to forgive her sins, come into her life, and be her Savior. That day she prayed to accept Jesus personally, and later at my home she received the baptism of the Holy Spirit, speaking in her prayer language.

A young man came to my house with deep wounds and hurts. He loved his wife and wanted the marriage to work. However, she would not cooperate. I spoke to him out of God's Word. It was evident that he didn't know Jesus personally. Two of the scriptures I gave him were Romans 3:23, "For all have sinned and come short of the glory of God," and Romans 6:23, "The wages of sin is death, but the gift of God is eternal life through Jesus Christ our Lord." He prayed to accept Jesus personally. Then I told him about Acts chapter two. "When the day of Pentecost was fully come, they were all with one accord in one place. And suddenly there came a sound from heaven of a rushing mighty wind, and it filled all the house where they were sitting, and there appeared unto them cloven tongues, like as of fire, and it sat upon each of them. And they were all filled with the Holy Ghost, and began to speak with tongues, as the Spirit gave them utterance" (KJV.) The Amplified Bible translates "tongues" as "different foreign languages."

"Would you like to give your life to Jesus and be filled with the Holy Spirit?" I asked him.

"Yes, I would," he replied. As he began to praise God, he spoke in a beautiful language he had not learned. A short time later, he and his wife were reunited and developed a more wonderful and loving relationship.

Some time later, another young man and his wife came for prayer because they were having problems in their marriage. The lady was saved, but he was not. He prayed to accept Jesus personally, received the Holy Spirit, and spoke in his heavenly language.

One afternoon I walked to the house of a lady who was an invalid after being inflicted with severe wounds by a robber. We conversed for a while. She acknowledged that she had never given her life to God. I presented the plan of salvation, and she prayed to accept Jesus personally. Her teenage granddaughter also repeated the prayer.

On another occasion, I visited a lady who had lost her son to a drug overdose. She was grieving greatly but then realized she needed Jesus to get through the crisis. Standing outside her home, she listened to me talk about the love of Jesus. She prayed to accept Jesus as her personal Savior.

One spring day, my granddaughter Crystal took me into town. I wanted to go to several houses and tell them about the love and power of God. "For God so loved the world, that He gave His only begotten Son, that whosoever believeth in Him should not perish, but have everlasting life," John 3:16. John 3:17 then tells us that God's Son didn't come to condemn, but to save. The echo was still there, loud and clear, "My assignment...Use every available opportunity."

A niece, her adult daughter, and her uncle's wife each prayed to accept Jesus personally. Another of her relatives also asked Jesus to be her personal Savior. That was a blessed day!

A young lady was in the hospital. The doctors gave her only a short time to live. I couldn't make it to the hospital to see her. So, one day, her aunt and some other relatives were visiting her and called me from the hospital. I asked the aunt to pray with the young lady to receive Jesus personally. The aunt had a suggestion. She said, "I will give her the phone and let you talk to her."

I addressed the young lady and said, "Would you like to ask Jesus to be your Savior?"

"Yes," she answered loudly and clearly. She prayed the sinner's prayer. Afterwards, she laughed loudly with joy and great enthusiasm. A few days later, she was gone.

Some may ask, "Will everyone who prays the sinner's prayer change their ungodly lifestyle and live for God?" The answer is no! Sometimes you may not see a change in their behavior. So, let's talk about those who really wanted a change and how I reached out to the seemingly neglected.

Chapter 22

REACHING FAR AND IN BETWEEN

Two mentally handicapped brothers lived together. One could do odd jobs and took care of his brother. I was a little fearful of entering their home. *Will I be able to explain the plan of salvation to them?* Neither had finished grade school. However, I realized that God is no respecter of persons. He wants all to be saved. "The Lord is not slack concerning His promise, as some men count slackness; but is longsuffering to us-ward, not willing that any should perish, but that all should come to repentance," 2 Peter 3:9.

One day when I visited their home, they welcomed me in. They were not strangers. I had known them for several years. Therefore, I was not afraid of them harming me. When I witness alone, I don't always enter a person's house. I usually witness outside.

I presented the plan of salvation. They both immediately prayed to accept Jesus Christ personally. They both lived several more years. The one who did odd jobs gave offerings to the church. One could say they were wonderful role models. Several young men would do well to follow their examples. God uses those who are willing to follow Him.

A lady and her husband lived out of state. I learned that he had a terminal disease. At the other end of the phone, he stated that he wanted to give his life to Jesus Christ. Later, he gave the phone to his wife, and she also prayed to accept Jesus. There was so much joy in the man's voice. A short time later, he departed this life.

One Friday night, during children's Bible study, the children responded to the class more than usual. Pastor Taylor asked me to pray with the children. There were several children between seven and twelve years of age. I whispered to each child, and each child stated that he or she wanted to accept Jesus as personal Savior. They prayed to accept Jesus.

Some might say that these children were too young. I beg to differ. My son told my mother that he wanted to give his life to Jesus when he was only seven years old. My mother led him in a prayer to accept Jesus as his personal Savior. He proved that he was for real.

I was still enthusiastic about "My Assignment," worked diligently, and used every available opportunity. One day between Sunday School and morning worship, I approached a middle-aged man who visited several churches but had never committed his life to Jesus Christ. I presented the plan of salvation and asked if he wanted to give his life to Jesus Christ. He slowly agreed. I admit that I was persuasive. Before you judge me or I judge myself, let's ask ourselves, how many times have we been persuasive in asking someone to see a movie or go someplace exciting? Later, at the proper time, I asked the man to stand up during the morning worship service and tell the audience about his salvation. He stood up and made the announcement.

The next Sunday, the man was back, but seemed very angry. He mumbled something to me. The word I heard was, "I want to talk to you." However, he never said any more, and he continued with his old lifestyle and addictions. I will still admit that I was a little anxious. However, I have this burning desire within to see people saved. I don't think it's me. I believe the Holy Spirit placed this desire within me. Jesus was rejected by many when He was on earth. Yet, He never gives up on us, as long as there is life in our bodies. "But God demonstrated His love toward us, in that while we were yet sinners, Christ died for us," Romans 5:8.

Where Two Roads Met

I stood in the middle of the roads and beckoned for a middle-aged lady to come to me. She owned a business and had a lot of influence over people, especially young adults. "May I talk with you?" I asked.

She smiled and answered, "Yes!"

I told her that God had a wonderful plan for her life. "For I know the thoughts that I think toward you, saith the Lord, thoughts of peace, and not of evil, to give you an expected end," Jeremiah 29:11. She listened attentively. "Would you like to give your life to the Lord and follow His plans for your life?" I asked.

"Yes," she answered with a smile. She then prayed to accept Jesus personally.

My church was conducting a revival at that particular time. I asked the lady to come that night. She came, still smiling. However, I never saw her in any church again, except at a funeral. Her business is still in operation, and she shows no signs of letting go of her old lifestyle. She is, therefore, in my daily prayers.

Follow-Up?

It is difficult to do a follow-up on some people because most will tell you they belong to a church, one they've been a member of since childhood. However, many of them haven't attended in years. Some attend on a regular basis, but will say that they have never asked Jesus to forgive their sins, come into their lives, and be their Savior. Their lifestyles are no different from those who have never connected to a church fellowship. Nevertheless, I believe the Lord has shown me a way to do some follow-up through writing. I will refer to this later in the book.

One year, I was asked to speak at an annual homecoming service in a particular town. I knew a lot of the people and that many of them did not profess to be Christians. As I began my message, I felt led by the Holy Spirit to make an altar call. All could remain at their seats but repeat the prayer to accept Jesus personally. "Lord, I am a sinner. I have never asked You to forgive my sins, come into my life, and be my Savior. I ask You now, forgive my sins, come into my life, and be my Savior. Thank You for coming into my life. I will read Your Word and follow You." This was the essence of the prayer.

Another time, I spoke at a small church. After my message, I made an altar call for those who wanted special prayer. Several people came up. I asked each, "What is your request?"

Thirteen replied, "I want to give my life to God." They prayed to accept Jesus personally.

Our church had a nursing home ministry, and I was placed over the ministry. Each time I spoke, I made an altar call. Remember the echo, "My Assignment." *Use every opportunity available to witness of the saving grace of Jesus Christ.* Later, I witnessed to two elderly men, and they prayed to accept Jesus.

I moved to my present location and joined my son Reverend Mark P. Forrest's church. Each time the opportunity presents itself I ask someone if they know Jesus Christ personally. If the answer is no, I ask them if they would like to invite Jesus to be their Savior. The answer is usually, "Yes!"

My greatest joy is being an altar worker. There is no greater ministry for me. The Bible says the angels rejoice when someone gives his or her life to Jesus Christ. My second greatest joy is writing. I have found that this is a great "follow-up ministry." Each month, a small staff and I publish a periodical entitled *The Inspirational/Amazing Thoughts.* This periodical contains excerpts of sermons by pastors, ministers, or other Christian leaders. It also features Bible puzzles and sometimes poems or "Golden Nuggets," a short encouraging phrase. The booklet also contains a plea and a prayer to accept Jesus as personal Savior.

Sometimes, I still witness by phone. The echo remains with me, and it is more powerful now than in the beginning, "My Assignment!" I must use every available opportunity to tell others about the love and power of God! Jesus is coming back one day. "Every eye shall see Him…" Revelation 1:7.

> "…Jesus Shall be revealed from heaven with His mighty angels, in flaming fire taking vengeance on them that know not God, and obey not the gospel of our Lord Jesus Christ: Who shall be punished with everlasting destruction from the presence of the Lord, and from the glory of His power. When He shall come to be glorified with His saints…" 2 Thessalonians 1:7-9.

> "He that overcometh shall inherit all things; I will be his God, and he shall be My son. But the fearful, and unbeliev-

ing, and the abominable, and murderers, and whoremongers, and sorcerers, and idolaters, and all liars, shall have their part in the lake which burneth with fire and brimstone..." Revelation 21:7-8.

Only those who accept Jesus personally and follow His teachings in the Bible will go to live with Him eternally in heaven's paradise. Those who neglect or reject Jesus will live eternally in a fiery hell.

God loves all of us. He sent His Son Jesus to die in our place so that we may have eternal life. He pleads to the unsaved, often through us saved believers in Christ Jesus, to give their lives to God and to live for Him.

You may say that some of those you witnessed to didn't live up to their confession of accepting Jesus Christ personally. We have to leave that to the work of the Holy Spirit. We are sent to witness. So let's always praise Him for the opportunity. As long as a person is alive, let's not give up hope. In the next chapter, you will find some more gems.

Chapter 23

HOPE FOR THE DESERT

At the close of chapter twenty-one, the question was asked, "Did all those who prayed to accept God personally turn away from practicing sin and live a godly lifestyle?" The answer is no, not right away. Some started practicing their Christian faith later. There are others in whom I haven't seen or heard of any lifestyle changes for Christ Jesus. But I still have hope. Let's talk about some of them.

First, let's talk about a few verses in Isaiah 35:3, 5-6 "Strengthen ye the weak hands, and confirm the feeble knees. The eyes of the blind shall be opened, and the ears of the deaf shall be unstopped. Then shall the lame leap as an hart, and the tongue of the dumb sing: for in the wilderness shall water break out, and streams in the desert. There is "Hope in the Desert!"

Even though the above scriptures were written before the birth of Jesus into this world, His death on a cruel cross for the sins of the world, and His ascension back to heaven, I believe the scriptures have a spiritual meaning for today. The following examples are still on my prayer list.

A lady talked to me about her brother who was critically ill in the hospital. She said that his conversation and lifestyle were ungodly. He didn't attend church or talk about Jesus. He was over fifty years of age. One day, while she was visiting him in the hospital, she called and asked me to pray with her brother to accept Jesus personally. She gave her brother the phone. I asked, "Do you want to give your life to the Lord?"

"Yes," he said, and prayed to accept Jesus. He was released from the hospital a short time later. But, I never heard or saw any evidence of him living for God. His sister now says that he never goes to church or talks about the Lord. It is as if he never prayed to accept Jesus personally, which was approximately three years ago. He is, yet, on my prayer list, and I pray for him daily that he will really give his life to the Lord.

God only told me to present His plan for salvation. I don't have the power to save. God has all power, but we must choose him. He knocks on the door, but we must open the door. "Behold, I (Jesus) stand at the door, and knock: if any man hears My voice, and opens the door, I will come in to him, and will sup with him, and he with Me," Revelation 3:20. The Amplified Bible says, "Behold, I (Jesus) stand at the door and knock; if any one hears and listens to and heeds My voice and opens the door, I will come in to him and will eat with him, and he [will eat] with Me." This is spiritual food. This is fellowship with God now and throughout eternity.

One day I asked a cousin to stop by my house. He came and blew his truck horn. Outside, leaning against his truck, I told him about the love of Jesus. He was a member of a church, but his lifestyle did not portray that of a Christian. Even his friends would laugh and say he enjoyed the clubs and things that the ungodly do. He prayed to accept Jesus personally.

Even though my cousin attends church, that old lifestyle is still there. Around Christians he talks about God, but his lifestyle and talk do not match. I, therefore, have not stopped praying for him.

A young man cried over the telephone because he was about to lose his job. He prayed to accept Jesus personally. After some negotiations, he was able to keep his job. However, he returned to his old style of living apart from God's instructions found in His word. "Take fast hold of instructions; let her not go: keep her for she is thy life. Enter not in the way of the wicked, and go not in the way of the evil man," Proverbs 4:3-4.

"The wages of sin is death, but the gift of God is eternal life, through Jesus Christ, our Lord," Romans 6:23. The wages or pay for sin is eternal death, separation from God in a fiery, burning hell. However, the gift of God is eternal life—life forever in paradise with God. The choice is ours.

I had completed "My Assignment" in that area. *What then? The best is yet to come!*

Chapter 24

ENJOYING THE SPECTACULAR

As I grew older, it appeared that God had rekindled my spiritual fire. He began to perform spectacularly. *Lord is this what you want me to do? But these old people are set in their ways. Will they become offended if I present the plan of salvation to them?* Nevertheless the urge was there.

I had witnessed to countless people, but these people seemed different. These elderly people lived in the same house with relatives. They seldom attended church services and appeared to have no room for God. I approached the younger person first and spoke of the wonderful works of Almighty God.

"'All have sinned and come short of the glory of God,' Romans 3:23 says." No response. I continued. "'…The wages of sin is death, but the gift of God is eternal life through Jesus Christ our Lord,' Romans 6:23 says." Still no response. "God has a wonderful plan and purpose for your life. Would you like to ask Jesus to forgive your sins, come into your life, and be your Savior?" I asked.

"Yes!" was the joyful response. Then the forgiveness from sin and the acceptance of Jesus as personal Savior was prayed. I wanted to shout for joy, but not yet. There was another "likely candidate" in the next room.

When I approached the other person, the sour look on his face did not deter me. Instead, a cautious boldness arose within me, and I continued. I repeated some of the same scriptures, but at times, he seemed preoccupied. However, I felt led of the Holy Spirit to continue. Eventually, he too prayed to accept Jesus personally. While he appeared to be happy, I was overjoyed.

Later, when I was at home alone, tears of joy flooded my soul. Yes, it is better to accept Jesus Christ at a young age. But, the love of God is so great that His heart is still tender, and His hands reach out to all ages. "…God demonstrated His love toward us, in that, while we were yet sinners, Christ died for us," Romans 5:8.

Then, the "Great Spectacular!" He was ninety-one years of age. To him, church was something nice and an intelligent place, but did he really know Jesus personally? There was no evidence. One day, I approached him. He had no recollection of accepting Jesus as his personal Savior long ago. Although he was now in the early stages of dementia, he remembered going to church since childhood. However, there was never a time when he earnestly believed that he was a sinner and asked Jesus to forgive his sins, come into his life, and be his Savior.

Fortunately, that day, inner amazing joy filled both of us as he gave his life to Jesus Christ. I informed him that he could be filled with the Holy Spirit and speak in his heavenly language, one he had not learned. For about thirty minutes, I sat quietly as he spoke in his heavenly language.

Was that spectacular? Yes, definitely! God performs the "Spectacular" in us and invites Himself to the celebration!

Chapter 25

A TIME FOR ENCOURAGEMENT

I sold my place in my hometown Collins, Georgia, because my daughter Annette had passed away, and my son Mark wanted to be able to take care of certain aspects of business in my older age. I lived with him and his wife Kelly for a while, but we each needed our "space." There was a nice apartment complex about one-and-a-half miles from their home, so I selected a nice two-bedroom apartment. They were there to see that my needs were met. There were a lot of families with children who lived there, and I enjoyed the atmosphere. However, Mark's father lived in a new adorable independent living facility, and he wanted us to live close together. His father and I had gone our separate ways years earlier, and it was not feasible to become husband and wife again. He was in poor health and needed special care, and I assisted in a great way.

Now he lives on the first floor, and my apartment is on the second floor. They are awesome living conditions. But, I miss the families with children. Since my apartment is in the front, every so often, I hear and see emergency vehicles pull up. They come into the building and take the sick, and sometimes the deceased, out on stretchers.

The Lord spoke to me about creating and conducting a time for encouragement. In fact the program is entitled, "A Time for Encouragement." Administration thought the idea was great and gave me permission to implement it. I discovered that the program was for me, also. Instead of focusing on who goes out on stretchers, for whatever reason, we enjoy reading and studying

God's wonderful Word. All the participants are seniors, but each has so much to give. I receive so much rich information. I feel like I am seated among many college professors.

Each time we do "Scenarios," they are based on God's Word. All are great with their acting abilities. I think some could have starred in movies and become as great as Cicely Tyson, James Earl Jones, Morgan Freeman, or Esther Rolle. The information doesn't remain stagnant. We wisely pass it on to our children and grandchildren.

Each day, I thank God for the privilege to serve. Want to hear about my other assignment? Read on

Chapter 26

SNACKS PLEASE!

Allow me to tell you about my wonderful and amazing church assignments. My first assignment is one of serving snacks after church. I enjoy this assignment almost as much as any other. Each Sunday, I arrive early so that a pot of coffee can start brewing. Sometimes the Director of Operations, Deacon Burch, races me to it. He is seventy years of age, but I am much older. I really enjoy serving snacks to everyone after the morning worship service. It gives me great joy.

I also have an assignment as superintendent of the Sunday School department and select teachers. They are some of the best. Shouts ring out and laughter is heard while we explore each lesson. It's an honor to serve.

Altar work, another one of my assignments, is close to my heart. Some want to give their lives to the Lord and be filled with His Holy Spirit. Pastor Mark Forrest accepts the honor but often delegates me or another altar worker to assist him.

Let me tell you about Christine. She accepted Jesus as her personal Savior and wanted to be filled with the Holy Spirit and receive her heavenly prayer language, as they did on the day of Pentecost in Acts chapter two. We always inform new converts that the heavenly language is not one they can learn. It is given to them by the Holy Spirit. Most of the people I have had the privilege of working with only speak English, but it was different with Christine. She was Hispanic and spoke both English and Spanish. I carefully informed her that the language the Holy Spirit was going to give her was not one she had learned. It was a heavenly language.

Christine began praising the Lord. It appeared that she wanted all the gifts God had for her. Within five minutes, she began speaking in a beautiful language. As tears rolled down her light tan cheeks, she shouted, "It's wonderful! It's wonderful!" The Holy Spirit assured me that she had indeed received the baptism of the Holy Spirit and her heavenly language. *Was this a snack?* This time, a heavenly perpetual meal—more than a snack—was received.

Unlike Christine, I wasn't sure if Erb was for real. Her body was laced with tattoos, but she was there each Sunday with other ladies. One Sunday, she went to Pastor Forrest for prayer. He then called me up and told me to work with her. I heard the Holy Spirit tell me to lead her into receiving the baptism of the Holy Spirit. *But, does she really want the heavenly language? She is only about twenty years old. Is she for real?* Soon after, I was reminded that the Holy Spirit did not make me a judge. He was in control.

"Would you like to receive the baptism of the Holy Spirit, speaking in your heavenly language?" I asked.

"Yes," Erb replied. She began praising the Lord, and within a few minutes she was speaking in a beautiful heavenly language. It was a language she had not learned. She paid no attention to the stares of other young people. She continued praising God. Another "snack" had become a perpetual, spiritual meal. And the list goes on with more young adults accepting Jesus as Lord and Savior and receiving their heavenly language. So, the coffee and snacks served at the end of church service is just a token of a greater meal, an ETERNAL FEAST served by the Holy Spirit!

Chapter 27

EXAMPLES OF PRESENTING
THE PLAN OF SALVATION

Some may say there are strategies in presenting the plan of salvation. I would like to say that my training came from great teachers and evangelists, like Dr. Bill Bright and Dr. Billy Graham. They wrote books, pamphlets, and tracts about their witnessing and allowed the Holy Spirit to lead them. They also listed key scriptures. You will notice the approach I made before presenting the plan of salvation and/or informed them about the baptism of the Holy Spirit. Mistakes were made, but the Holy Spirit led me through them while instructing me.

The baptism of the Holy Spirit with evidence of speaking in an unlearned language is found in Acts 2:1-4 and 1 Corinthians chapters 12 and 14. The Holy Spirit lists different ministering gifts in 1 Corinthians chapter 12.

Examples of a few people who received the baptism of the Holy Spirit, not previously mentioned, are included in this chapter. Two people Jesus witnessed to come near the close of this book.

Example #1: Pearlie and Mae

Mae was a neighbor and loved by most people. However, others and myself knewby her lifestyle that she didn't know Jesus personally. Mae was a faithful member of a church. How do you approach someone like this and present the plan of salvation? I had a strong urge and decided to follow my urge.

The Dialogue

Pearlie: Mae, do you know Jesus personally? Have you ever given your life to Him?

Mae: Sure! I am a Christian!

Pearlie: Share your experience with me. How did it happen?

Mae: I became a member of my church and was baptized when I was a teenager. I married, had
two children, and took them to church. They are grown. I have been faithful to my
church.

Pearlie: The Bible says in Romans 3:23, "All have sinned and come short of the glory of God."

Ephesians 2:8-9 says, "For by grace are you saved through faith, and that not of yourselves: it is the gift of God: not of works lest any man should boast."

Isaiah 64:6 says, "All our righteousness is as filthy rags." I am not saved because of my "good works," but because I asked Jesus to forgive my sins, come into my life, and be my Savior.

Mae: Is that the way it is?

Pearlie: Have you ever told God that you are sorry for your sins, asked Him to come into your life and be your Savior?

Mae: No! I have not!

Pearlie: Would you like to ask Him to come into your life and be your Savior?

Mae: Yes! I would!

Pearlie: Please repeat this prayer after me, "Lord God, in Jesus' name, I have sinned. Forgive my sins, come into my life and be my Savior."

Mae repeated the prayer. Later, she was filled with The Holy Spirit and spoke in her prayer language, one she had not learned. Her lifestyle has changed from ungodliness to that of a Christian. Years later, she is still strong in the Lord.

EXAMPLE #2 - Pearlie and Neaka

I was a tutor for afterschool at-risk students in my section of the county. Some were not at-risk but still wanted to come and were permitted to do so. Neaka, a beautiful young lady and high school senior, mostly distanced herself from other students. I tried to involve her in academics and sports, but the progress was slow. She mostly gave excuses.

The Dialogue

Pearlie: Neaka, would you like to be a part of this skit?

Neaka: No, Ms. Forrest.

One day, several students and I sat around a long table. They took turns reading a story. It came Neaka's turn to read. She was silent.

Pearlie: Neaka, will you read?

Neaka: My teachers will not let me read.

Neaka would not participate in sports. She would stand or sit around, smile, and watch the other students participate. One day, Neaka got off the bus and walked into the classroom with a very sad face. She put her book bag on her desk and immediately walked to my desk.

Neaka: Ms. Forrest, may I talk to you privately?
Pearlie: Yes. (I left another student in charge, and Neaka and I walked outside).
Neaka: I am quitting school. (Tears rolled down her beautiful tan face).
Pearlie: Why? You will graduate in less than six months.
Neaka: I am tired of being called stupid! Everybody says I'm stupid!
Pearlie: Neaka, you are not stupid! You have talents and can do a lot of good things. You are kind. You care about people. You have a beautiful singing voice. You can learn and you are learning.
Neaka: I can learn?
Pearlie: Yes! You can learn! God loves you. He will help you learn a lot more. Do you know Jesus personally?
Neaka: No.
Pearlie: Would you like to give Him your life? He'll be your friend, forever.
Neaka: Yes!
Pearlie: Please pray this prayer after me. "Father God, in Jesus' name, forgivemy sins, come into my life, and be my Savior." (A big smile lit up Neaka's face).
Pearlie: I will be at you graduation. I will watch as you walk across that stage and receive your diploma.

After our little talk, until graduation, Neaka had a better attitude. She even participated in more activities. A few months later, I watched as she walked across the stage and received her high school diploma.

EXAMPLE #3 - Pearlie, Mrs. Emie, Ethel, and Jade

It was Saturday night after 11:00 P.M. My sister Ethel was preparing to leave my house. We both were scheduled to be at Sunday School at 9:00 A.M. the next day. My telephone rang and I picked up the receiver.

The Dialogue

Pearlie: Hello!

Ernie: This is Emie. My daughter Jade says she is ready to get saved. I am at her house now. Can you come to her house?

Pearlie: Just a moment. Ethel, can you take me to Jade's house? Emie says Jade is ready to give her life to the Lord.

Ethel: Praise the Lord! Sure, I'll take you!

About ten minutes later, we were at Jade's house. She invited us into her living room.

Pearlie: Jade, would you like to accept Jesus as your personal Savior and be filled with the Holy Spirit?

Jade: Yes! I am ready!

Pearlie: Romans 10:13 says, "For whosoever shall call upon the name of the Lord shall be saved.

Acts chapter two tells us that a group of people were together, waiting to be filled with the Holy Spirit. Suddenly, the Holy Spirit came upon each of them and they were filled with the Holy Spirit and spoke in languages they had not learned. We call it a "special prayer language." Are you ready?

> **Jade:** Yes! I am!
>
> **Pearlie:** Please repeat a prayer after me. At the end of the prayer, begin praising God by saying, "Hallelujah! Hallelujah! Hallelujah," until you are no longer speaking in your own language, but your heavenly language. Please repeat, "Father God, in Jesus' name, forgive my sins, come into my life and be my Savior. Fill me with Your Holy Spirit." (Jade repeated the prayer).
>
> **Jade:** Hallelujah! Hallelujah! Hallelujah!...

Ethel and I continued to pray with her and encourage her. "Don't give up!" we said. Just when we thought we would have to come back another time, Jade began speaking in her heavenly language. She praised God and so did her mother Emie.

Jade and her children moved to another state with her mother. However, Emie continued to visit her sister who lived near me. On one of those visits, Emie brought Jade's two preteen-aged children to see me.

"Jade said that she wants her children to get saved before returning home," Emie said. I led the children in a prayer to receive Jesus as their personal Savior. TO GOD BE THE GLORY!

Chapter 28

THE MASTER SOUL WINNER:

JESUS AND NICODEMUS (JOHN 3)

Nicodemus: Rabbi, we know that Thou art a teacher come from God: for no man can do these miracles that Thou doest, except God be with him.

Jesus: Verily, verily, (Truly, truly) I say unto thee, except a man be born again, he cannot see the kingdom of God.

Nicodemus: How can a man be born when he is old? Can he enter the second time into his mother's womb, and be born?

Jesus: Verily, verily, I say unto thee, except a man be born of water and of the Spirit, he cannot enter the kingdom of God. That which is born of flesh is flesh; and that which is born of Spirit is spirit. Marvel not that I said unto thee, ye must be born again. The wind bloweth where it listeth, and thou hearest the sound thereof, but canst not tell whence it cometh, and whither it goeth: so is everyone that is born of the Spirit.

Nicodemus: How can these things be?

Jesus: Art thou a master of Israel, and knowest not these things? Verily, verily, I say unto thee, we speak that we do know, and testify that we have seen; and we receive not our witness.

If I have told you earthly things, and ye receive not, how shall ye believe, if I tell you of heavenly things? And no man hath ascended up heaven, but He that came down from heaven, even the Son of man which is in heaven. And as Moses lifted up the serpent in the wilderness, even so must the Son of man be lifted up: that whosoever believeth in Him, should not perish, but have eternal life. But God so loved the world, that He gave His only begotten Son, that whosoever believeth in Him should not perish, but have everlasting life.

The Results

John 19:38-42, tell us when Jesus died on the cross, Joseph of Arimathaea and Nicodemus took the body of Jesus, prepared Him for burial, and put Him in a new sepulcher (tomb). After Jesus was buried, He arose three days later and stayed on the earth forty days. He ascended back to heaven, is seated at the right hand of Father God, and is making intercession for us. He is preparing a place for "born again" believers to be with Him forever and forever.

Jesus, the greatest soul winner, teaches us by his Holy Spirit how to witness so that others can be saved!

Chapter 29

JESUS AND THE SAMARITAN WOMAN (JOHN 4)

Jesus and His disciples left Judea for Galilee. The Jews had no dealings with the Samaritans. They were outcasts. So, the Jews found a way to bypass Samaria. As they traveled on this particular day, Jesus told His disciples that He must go through Samaria. They came to the city of Sychar in Samaria. It was noon. Jesus was tired and sat on "Jacob's well." In the meantime, His disciples went into the city to buy food. A Samaritan woman came to the well to draw water. Jesus then asked her for some water.

The Dialogue

Jesus: Give me to drink.

Samaritan Woman: How is it that Thou, being a Jew, asketh drink of me, which am a woman of Samaria? For the Jews have no dealings with the Samaritans.

Jesus: If thou kneweth the gift of God, and who it is that said to thee, give me to drink; thou wouldest have asked of Him, and He would have given thee living water.

Samaritan Woman: Sir, Thou hast nothing to draw with, and the well is deep: from whence then hast Thou that living water? Art Thou greater than our father Jacob, which gave us the well, and drank thereof himself, and his children, and his cattle.

Jesus: Whosoever drinketh of this water shall thirst again: But whosoever drinketh of the water that I shall give him shall never thirst; but the water that I shall give him shall be in him a well of water springing up into everlasting life.

Samaritan Woman: Sir, give me this water, that I thirst not, neither come here to draw.

Jesus: Go, call your husband, and come hither.

Samaritan Woman: I have no husband.

Jesus: Thou hast well said, I have no husband; for thou hast had five husbands; and he whom thou now hast is not thy husband: in that saidst thou truly.

Samaritan Woman: Sir, I perceive that Thou art a prophet. Our fathers worshipped in this mountain; and Ye say, that Jerusalem is the place where men ought to worship.

Jesus: Woman, believe Me, the hour cometh, when ye shall neither in this mountain, nor yet at Jerusalem, worship the Father. Ye worship ye know not what: we know what we worship: for salvation is of the Jews. But the hour cometh, and now is, when the true worshippers shall worship the Father in Spirit and in truth: For the Father seeketh such to worship Him. God is a Spirit: and they that worship Him must worship Him in spirit and in truth.

Samaritan Woman: I know that Messias cometh, which is called Christ: when He cometh, He will tell us all things.

Jesus: I that speak unto thee am He. (Jesus' disciples came and marveled that He talked with the woman. But they didn't ask any questions).

Samaritan Woman: (She left her water pots and went into the city. She spoke to the men). Come see a man, which told me all things that ever I did: Is not this the Christ?

The Results

Jesus gave the Samaritan woman new life. She then told others about her new life. The city went out to see Jesus. The "Revival" continued for two days, and many became followers of Jesus Christ.